The 2

End-Times

WARS

for the
Jewish People

By Wendy Bowen

MANIFEST
PUBLICATIONS

Manifest International, LLC

ISBN: 978-0-692-99881-6

Scripture references in this book are from the New
International Version of the Bible unless otherwise noted.
Bold emphasis and bracketed notes inside Biblical texts were
added by author for teaching purposes.

Scripture taken from the HOLY BIBLE, NEW
INTERNATIONAL VERSION ® NIV ® Copyright © 1973,
1978, 1984, 2011 by Biblica, Inc. Used by permission of
Biblica, Inc. All rights reserved worldwide.

Editing: Katherine Bell
Cover Design: Don Patton
Stormy Sky Photo Credit: Freepik

CONTENTS

FOREWORD

To the Jewish people of all nations,

I write this to you because I love God, and God loves you. I write this because I love you, and it is my desire that you not miss out on your Jewish inheritance in this world or in the world to come. You are God's chosen people, and I have been praying for you for years while trusting that ALL of God's prophecies and promises for you will come to pass. After an extended time in Jerusalem which was devoted to prayer and seeking God for wisdom, I am writing this book because I believe it to be God's heart reaching out for your attention in this day and for your protection in the times to come.

There are two great wars which are already in motion and will be ever-increasing until Messiah comes to judge all things: the War in This World and the War for Your Soul. These conflicts bring unique challenges and blessings to you as God's chosen people, to Israel, and to God's Kingdom. In this book, we are going to investigate the Scriptures and what the Prophets of God have said as it pertains to the way that God handles matters with the Jewish people, with Gentile nations, and what His plans and purposes are for His eternal Kingdom.

God is a holy God—the only Creator of the Universe. As such, He has Sovereign authority over all the nations of the earth. This means that He can plant them or pluck them up, build them up or overthrow them. (See Jeremiah 1:10.) This is true whether the nations know it or not and whether they acknowledge Him as God or not. Until Messiah comes to judge this world and usher in the world to come, God orchestrates international affairs among the nations with righteousness and justice and does so in accordance with the ways He has revealed in the Scriptures. Of course, this includes His unfailing love and faithfulness toward the Jewish people, in keeping with His covenants with you.

This said, anyone with any measure of experience in interpreting Biblical prophecy knows the various challenges of undertaking such a task. It often seems easier to just wait until a prophecy is fulfilled to see how God causes His written word to come to pass in a way that precisely matches the Biblical text. I have heard it said that interpreting Biblical prophecy is like gazing upon a mountain range from a distance: One discerns that there are different mountains and that some are larger or smaller or closer or farther. But, it can be difficult to discern the sequence and order of the mountains, and it can be difficult to tell whether some of the mountains appear to be smaller simply because they are farther away. Those things can only be known when one is in the midst of the mountain range. Until then, it is often a matter of perspective.

As such, I have done my best to assemble the most significant and relevant highlights from the Scriptures as a guide for our study. My aim has been to keep this book short and to the point so it is impossible to include all of the Scriptures that support my case. Therefore, I implore you to finish reading this short book in its entirety and once you have read it, take the necessary steps to do your own research. Seek only the truth, and confirm the facts for yourself.

Before you begin reading, ask God to enlighten your understanding, grant you revelation of the truth, and help you follow Him and His words, wherever they may lead you. This book could change your perspective about God, your understanding of God's dealings with the Jewish people and the Gentile nations, and your outlook about the coming of Messiah. It could even change the course of your life. In fact, your life and your eternal soul depends on the decisions you make in your own heart and in your own mind about the matters presented in this book. You and I both stand eternally responsible for what is written on its pages.

So, let us begin. Let us reason together as we examine these things. And please, remember that I write this because my heart's desire is for you to be assured of your Jewish inheritance and become equipped to stand firm in it until you receive the fullness of God's Kingdom and His perfect shalom in the world to come.

Shalom and love,

Wendy Bowen

Jerusalem, Israel, 2017

Jeremiah 29:11-14 - For I know the plans I have for you," declares the LORD, "plans to prosper you and not to harm you, plans to give you hope and a future. Then you will call on me and come and pray to me, and I will listen to you. You will seek me and find me when you seek me with all your heart. I will be found by you," declares the LORD, "and will bring you back from captivity. I will gather you from all the nations and places where I have banished you," declares the LORD, "and will bring you back to the place from which I carried you into exile."

1

THE WAR IN THIS WORLD

Have you ever looked at Jewish history and wondered what in the world God was thinking?

Understanding how God has His hand in international affairs is particularly relevant for today because we are at a critical turning point in history. In fact, there is a great shaking coming to all the nations of the earth. Everything that can be shaken will be shaken. There will be economic and governmental collapse, famines and plagues, floods, tsunamis and strange tides, hurricanes, tornadoes, earthquakes, and many such things as these. There will be increasing violence, civil wars within nations, wars between nations, and wars of world powers fighting for domination of global resources. Just in case you are wearing rose-colored glasses or are otherwise unaware, these things are already happening in the world today and are increasing. Like a woman in labor whose contractions grow stronger and closer together before she gives birth, the tribulation in this world will increase in severity and frequency. Plus, even though I sincerely wish this were not the case, what lies ahead is worldwide persecution of the Jewish people, a global expulsion of the Jewish people from the nations in which they reside, and another holocaust of global proportions.

If you ask your rabbis about world events and Jewish history, you may or may not be satisfied with their answers. For example, it is commonly accepted among Jews that God judges Israel, the Jewish people, directly, and He judges Gentile nations by how they treat the Jewish people. Additionally, rabbis attribute the first exile of the Jewish people to "idolatry" and the second exile to "hatred without cause" or "causeless hatred" although none of these teachers seem to know exactly what this means or how it could justify two thousand years of wandering. Moreover, the rabbinic responses about international affairs and anti-Semitism are typically a recipe with a special mix of these ingredients, give or take depending on the rabbi. The recipe: one part suffering of the righteous Jews plus one part "us vs. the Gentiles," seasoned to taste with their own special mix of personal political leanings and business acumen, and garnished with a glance into the future when the Messiah comes to punish the whole world for its evil treatment of the Jewish people and establish peace on earth. Although these observations are true in part, they give us an incomplete, harsh, and mysterious picture of God's involvement with world events.

For example, consider the Book of Jonah. Nineveh, a Gentile city, was the largest city in the world in its time. God sent Jonah to warn the people of Nineveh that the wrath of God was coming to destroy them because of their sinful ways. But when the King of Nineveh called for national repentance with prayer and fasting, God relented of bringing disaster. However, about a century or so later, the people of Nineveh were back to their old ways and God's Prophet Nahum issued an irreversible decree of destruction. (See the Book of Nahum.) Nineveh was demolished and never rebuilt. Its ruins are the only thing remaining to testify that it ever existed.

When God brings judgment against any nation for its own sin or for its treatment of the Jewish people, He is perfectly justified in doing so. However, we must remember that God is abounding in mercy and sometimes delays for hundreds if not thousands of years to give plenty of time for people to change their ways— or not.

What you may not realize is that, similar to the story of Jonah and Nineveh, the Scriptures reveal to us from God's vantage point everything that has happened throughout history and all of the things that will continue to happen until the Messiah comes. God has known the end of the story from the beginning of time. Out of kindness to His beloved people, the Jews, He has spoken through His Prophets to tell us in advance about what is happening in the earth. God's Prophets have a track record for accuracy of one hundred percent. (See Amos 3:7.)

As we stand today, there are still significant events foretold by God's Prophets and promised to Israel which are yet to be fulfilled. However, as Israel's King Solomon said, there is nothing new under the sun. Everything that will happen has already happened.

Ecclesiastes 1:9-10 - ***What has been will be again,***

what has been done will be done again; *there is nothing new under the sun. Is there anything of which one can say, "Look! This is something new"?* ***It was here already, long ago; it was here before our time***.

Therefore, before we look to the future, we must look to the past. The history we are going to examine covers thousands of years and goes a little like this: God promised a land to Abraham and then his descendants moved to Egypt for four hundred years. Next, He delivered His people from Egypt and crushed the Egyptians. Then, God kicked the Amorites out of Canaan and gave their land as an inheritance to His people, Israel. Hundreds of years later, Gentile nations attacked and displaced the Jews from the Land that God had given them. Then, after a few generations, God called the Jews back to the Land and destroyed the Gentile nations which had dispersed them. After several intervals of anti-Semitic persecution and war, it appeared that the words of the Prophets were sufficiently fulfilled for the world to come to an end in the great and terrible Day of the LORD. But it didn't. Soon enough, Assyria and Babylon, Gentile empires, attacked the Jewish people, and the Jews were scattered to the four corners of the earth. In time, Assyria and Babylon plus every nation that had been unsupportive of the Jewish people ceased to exist. For two thousand years, the dispersed Jews wandered from nation to nation. History was filled with ebbs and flows of peace and prosperity for the Jews followed by persecution, decimation, and further displacement. There were Jewish taxations and trade restrictions, blood libels, inquisitions, crusades, pogroms, and expulsions followed by times of starting all over again. Then, after two thousand years of exile, Jews began returning to the Promised Land and settling there. As another round of horrible anti-Semitic persecution began brewing in Europe, Jews were consistently warned to flee for safety, but most did not. Then, the largest Jewish massacre in history took place during World War II when almost all of the nations of the world were fighting and almost none of the nations of the world supported the Jews. After this holocaust, the State of Israel was established in 1948 as the nation of Israel we know today. Now, Jews from all over the world have returned to the Promised Land and call Israel their home though many still remain scattered throughout the nations of the world. Next . . .

Ok. Let's go through this a little more slowly.

God's Sovereignty Over the Nations

When God chose Abraham, the founding father of the Jewish people, He called him out of Babylon. Abraham lived in Ur of the Chaldeans and God told him to get out of Babylon and go to a land that He would show him. God promised to give Abraham a land, a people, and make him a blessing to the whole world.

*Genesis 12:1-3 - The LORD had said to Abram, "**Go from your country, your people and your father's household to the land I will show you. I will make you into a great nation, and I will bless you; I will make your name great, and you will be a blessing**. I will bless those who bless you, and whoever curses*

5

you I will curse; **and all peoples on earth will be blessed through you**.*"*

Genesis 13:14-15 - The LORD said to Abram after Lot had parted from him, **"Look around from where you are [between Bethel and Ai], to the north and south, to the east and west. All the land that you see I will give to you and your offspring forever."**

Genesis 15:18-21 - On that day the LORD made a covenant with Abram and said, **"To your descendants I give this land, from the Wadi of Egypt to the great river, the Euphrates**--*the land of the Kenites, Kenizzites, Kadmonites, Hittites, Perizzites, Rephaites, Amorites, Canaanites, Girgashites and Jebusites."*

From the time that God entered into covenant with Abraham, He clearly communicated the reason why He could not give Abraham and his descendants the Promised Land right away. God plainly stated that the sin of the Amorites had not yet reached its full measure. ("Amorites" was the all-inclusive term used to describe the nations listed above.)

Genesis 15:13-16 - Then the LORD said to him [Abraham], *"Know for certain that* **for four hundred years your descendants will be strangers in a country not their own and that they will be enslaved and mistreated there**. *But* **I will punish the nation they serve as slaves,** *and afterward they will come out with great possessions. You, however, will go to your ancestors in peace and be buried at a good old age.* **In the fourth generation your**

6

descendants will come back here, for the sin of the Amorites has not yet reached its full measure."

This prophetic revelation given by God to Abraham includes insight into how God handled several international situations. God revealed to Abraham that the Amorites would be allowed to keep living in the Land for another four hundred or so years. Why? God could have given the Land to Abraham right then and there. But God is a merciful God and it would be against His good nature to severely punish any people or displace any nation until their wickedness merited such Sovereign intervention.

To illustrate this, think of one of those pictures of a thermometer that people use for fundraising to show how much money has been raised and how much funding remains to be raised. Until the thermometer is full, the project cannot move forward because funding is not complete. In God's dealing with nations, until their "sin thermometer" is full of collective and accumulated sin and wickedness, though it may take centuries to become full enough, destruction or expulsion is not yet in alignment with God's justice and mercy. The fact that sin and violence are allowed to remain in the world today is evidence of God's mercy toward even the worst offenders and that He takes no delight in crushing nations or in the death of the wicked. (See Ezekiel 18:23 and 33:11.) This said, as Judge of all the earth, He must execute righteous judgment when it is warranted.

To further this point, consider the fact that God did not even destroy Sodom and Gomorrah without sending angels to verify that their wickedness was bad enough to warrant it. Sodom and Gomorrah were cities which existed in Abraham's day and the outcry against them had reached up to heaven. The sin and lawlessness of Sodom and Gomorrah was so flagrant that the men of Sodom wanted to rape God's messengers for sexual pleasure. When Sodom and Gomorrah's destruction was certain, Abraham appealed to God's perfect sense of justice for the righteous people who lived in the cities. God made a way for Lot and his family, the only righteous ones in Sodom, to escape. When they had been escorted out of the city to safety, God rained down fire and sulfur, destroying Sodom, Gomorrah, and the surrounding cities until they became a wasteland. (See Genesis 19.)

However, in the days of Abraham, Isaac, and Jacob, the Amorite nations did not yet warrant such a judgment or expulsion from the Land. Therefore, the twelve tribes of Israel went to live in Egypt because of famine in the land of Canaan. At first, the Jews prospered there and multiplied greatly. But the rulers of Egypt ran a tight regime of domination and subjugation. The government owned all the land in Egypt, and the Egyptian people were enslaved to the government because they had sold their land and themselves as servants when there had been a worldwide famine. Conformity was commanded, and rebellion against the government was often met with violence or penalty of death. Therefore, when the Egyptian leaders saw the Jews excelling, they became concerned that the Jews would outnumber them, outsmart them, and overthrow them. Consequently, they subjected the Jews to harsh slavery under their dictatorial rule. In today's terms, this would be called discrimination, persecution, anti-Semitism, pogroms, and labor camps. This went on for over four hundred years. Please note that rabbis say that this went on for only two and a half centuries, but Scripture expressly says four hundred thirty years to the very day. (See Exodus 12:41.) Although it may seem that God was failing His people through neglect and apparent lack of intervention during this time, this was all in fulfillment of what God had revealed to Abraham from the start.

When the time foretold by God finally came, Egypt's wicked regime of oppression combined with their treatment of the Jews warranted this people's destruction and demise. God sent plagues of judgment as warnings against the Egyptians while protecting the Jewish people from the majority of these disasters. Finally, God delivered His people in what we now know of as the story of Passover (Pesach) and demolished Pharaoh and his Egyptian armies in the bottom of the sea. (See Exodus 1-14.) I believe that the only reason why Egypt was not completely destroyed and still exists as a nation today is to stand as a witness in the earth that these events did actually take place.

After leaving Egypt, the Israelites spent one year in the wilderness receiving the Torah and learning the ways of God. God was ready to give them the Promised Land. By this point in history, the sin of the Amorites had reached full measure and this warranted their destruction and expulsion from the Land promised to Abraham's descendants. However, the Israelites did not believe that God could give it to them, even though they had just seen with their own eyes what He had done to the Egyptians. Therefore, God decreed a forty-year delay. An entire generation of Israelites had to die in the wilderness before they could move forward and enter the Promised Land and the Amorites stayed in the land for forty years that they did not deserve. Finally, after forty years had passed, God gave power to a new generation of Israelites to conquer the Amorite nations. In spite of the fact that the Amorites were much larger, stronger, and more powerful than the Israelites, the Amorites didn't stand a chance because it was God who empowered His people.

Gentile Nations Judged and Destroyed

Because the sin of the Amorites had reached full measure, God told the Israelites not to offer any terms of peace to the Amorite nations, kingdoms, or cities within the boundaries of the Promised Land. His instructions were to utterly destroy them and show no mercy.

*Deuteronomy 7:2 - and when the LORD your God has delivered them [the Amorite nations] over to you and you have defeated them, **then you must destroy them totally. Make no treaty with them, and show them no mercy**.*

*Deuteronomy 20:16-18 - However, in the cities of the nations the LORD your God is giving you as an inheritance, **do not leave alive anything that breathes. Completely destroy them--the Hittites, Amorites, Canaanites, Perizzites, Hivites and Jebusites--as the LORD your God has commanded you.** Otherwise, they will teach you to follow all the* *detestable things they do in worshiping their gods, and you will sin against the LORD your God.*

In this case, God was using His people to displace the Amorites because of the Amorite wickedness. God made it clear that this was not because the Israelites had merited the Promised Land, nor was it because of their own righteousness. God was fulfilling His promise to Abraham, Isaac, and Jacob while simultaneously punishing the wickedness of the Amorites.

> *Deuteronomy 9:4-7 - After the LORD your God has driven them out before you, do not say to yourself, "The LORD has brought me here to take possession of this land because of my righteousness." **No, it is on account of the wickedness of these nations that the LORD is going to drive them out before you. It is not because of your righteousness or your integrity that you are going in to take possession of their land; but on account of the wickedness of these nations**, the LORD your God will drive them out before you, **to accomplish what he swore to your fathers, to Abraham, Isaac and Jacob**. Understand, then, that **it is not because of your righteousness that the LORD your God is giving you this good land to possess, for you are a stiff-necked people**. Remember this and never forget how you aroused the anger of the LORD your God in the wilderness. From the day you left Egypt until you arrived here, you have been rebellious against the LORD.*

Moreover, we must take note of the fact that the sin of the Amorites had nothing to do with their treatment of the Jewish people. This begs the question: What criteria was God using to judge the wickedness of the nations, kingdoms, and cities? What merited His judgment for their destruction and displacement if it was not in direct relation to their treatment of the Jewish people? Yes, God is Sovereign over all nations and can do whatever He pleases. However, if God displaced Amorite nations only because of His promise to Abraham to do so then God's character in His reasonable execution of justice as Judge of the whole earth is severely called into question. Fortunately, the Scriptures tell us plainly the reasons why Gentile nations were destroyed and expelled.

*Deuteronomy 18:9-14 - When you enter the land the LORD your God is giving you, do not learn to imitate the detestable ways of the nations there. Let no one be found among you who **sacrifices their son or daughter in the fire [kills innocent children for self-serving reasons], who practices divination or sorcery [seeking or accessing the spiritual or its powers through methods not prescribed in the Torah], interprets omens [fortune telling or interpreting events or circumstances as divine messages], engages in witchcraft [manipulation of people and events for a desired outcome], or casts spells [using spiritual methods to control people or situations], or who is a medium or spiritist [being or consulting with spiritual "gurus" or using New Age practices, hand of Fatima, yoga] or who consults the dead [raising the spirits of or consulting with those who are no longer in this world]**. Anyone who does these things is detestable* *to the LORD;* **because of these same detestable practices the LORD your God will drive out those nations before you.** *You must be blameless before the LORD your God. The nations you will dispossess* **listen to those who practice sorcery or divination [those who seek or access the spiritual or its powers through methods not prescribed in the Torah].** *But as for you, the LORD your God has not permitted you to do so.*

Leviticus 18:24-25 - [Pagan spiritual practices and sexually immoral practices including **incest, adultery, homosexuality, beastiality [sex with an animal], and killing innocent children**...] *"Do not defile yourselves in any of these ways,* **because this is how the nations that I am going to drive out before you became defiled. Even the land was defiled; so I punished it for its sin, and the land vomited out its inhabitants."** *(Please read the whole chapter of Leviticus 18 for yourself.)*

Ezekiel 16:49-50 - "Now this was the sin of your sister Sodom: She and her daughters were **arrogant, overfed and unconcerned; they did not help the poor and needy. They were haughty and did detestable things before me. Therefore I did away with them as you have seen.***"*

These passages, in addition to many others, reveal that all forms of unbiblical spirituality and false religion that does not adhere to the Torah; all forms of sexual immorality, which is any sexual activity outside of marriage between a man and his wife; prideful arrogance; apathy toward the poor; and other such sins are some of the reasons why nations are destroyed, overthrown, and removed from the earth. Let us also consider that when the whole world was participating in these types of activities in Noah's day, God sent a great flood to judge the whole earth while warning Noah and protecting him and his family from the destruction.

It is these types of offenses which fill up the "sin thermometer" of any nation until it reaches up to heaven. When it does, God sovereignly removes the nation's protection and ability to defend itself from enemy attacks.

> *Numbers 14:9 – [Joshua speaking] "Only do not rebel against the LORD. **And do not be afraid of the people of the land [the Amorites nations], because we will devour them. Their protection is gone, but the LORD is with us. Do not be afraid of them.**"*

While the nation's defenses are removed, God also empowers the nation's enemies to conquer them.

Jewish People Judged and Expelled

But what about Israel and the Jewish people? You may have heard that Gentiles will be Gentiles and will get what is coming to them, but Jews are special to God and looked upon by different criteria. You may have heard that all Jews are righteous in God's sight as the rabbis teach Isaiah 60:21 and are exempt from judgment for these types of things as the apple of God's eye. You may have heard that that Jewish suffering is the suffering of the righteous at the hands of angry, jealous, Gentile nations.

Yes, the Jewish people are special to God and were

chosen by Him out of all the nations of the earth. Yes, God does deal with the Jewish people differently than He does with other nations because of His covenant with them. But no, Jews are not all righteous in God's sight. The Isaiah passage in its proper context refers to a time when the Messiah reigns over all of the Jewish people. This has not happened yet. Moreover, King Solomon publicly confessed that all Jews sin. (See 1 Kings 8:46.) In fact, the Jewish people have violated the Torah and God's covenant with them many times and in many ways.

Read the following Scripture all the way through to the end. The first part of this saying of Moses is quoted frequently in Jewish prayers by many observant Jews all over the world. However, the rabbis have cut off the second part of the Scripture from Jewish prayer life and unfortunately, this has resulted in a skewed view of God's dealings with His own people.

*Exodus 34:6-7 - And he [the LORD] passed in front of Moses, proclaiming, "**The LORD, the LORD, the compassionate and gracious God, slow to anger, abounding in love and faithfulness, maintaining love to thousands, and forgiving wickedness, rebellion and sin. Yet he does not leave the guilty unpunished; he punishes the children and their children for the sin of the parents to the third and fourth generation**."*

*Deuteronomy 7:9-11 - Know therefore that the LORD your God is God; **he is the faithful God, keeping his covenant of love to a thousand generations of those who love him and keep his***

commandments. But those who hate him [as evidenced by their disobedience] he will repay to their face by destruction; he will not be slow to repay to their face those who hate him. *Therefore, take care to follow the commands, decrees and laws I give you today.*

Please hear me and do not doubt that God loves the Jewish people. No other nation on earth has a covenant with God except the Jewish people. Selah. He chose Israel to be special to Him and to be in covenant with Him. Therefore, God handles the Jewish people with more mercy and lovingkindness than all the other nations of the earth.

First of all, when God gave the Torah at Mount Sinai, as a mercy to His covenant people, He clearly laid out the consequences which would result for them if they did not obey His laws and statutes. The Torah outlines both the blessings for the Jewish people when they obey God and also the curses or consequences that will result from disobedience to the Torah. The curses of the Torah are written out fully in Leviticus Chapter 26 and Deuteronomy Chapter 28. These chapters include, but are not limited to, building wealth and having it taken from you, being "accident prone" or subject to senseless tragedies, every kind of physical sickness, mental illness and dysfunction, disasters which plummet business and family life, defeat and oppression by foreigners, terror and dread of enemies, exile to distant nations, and becoming an "object of horror" for all the world to see. I implore you to read these chapters in their entirety for yourself because the curses of the Torah remain in effect even to the third and fourth generation of those who violate God's rules and statutes. (See Exodus 34:7.) The point is that God did not make a mystery of Himself on these matters. Because of His great love for His people, He told them clearly from the beginning what would happen if they did not obey Him.

Along these lines, as a loving Father to the Jewish people, God warned His people when they sinned to a level that warranted the infliction of these curses upon them. He told them to stop doing the wrong things they were doing so that He would not have to institute the consequences for their actions. God, in His great mercy, sent His Prophets to tell His people to repent and to warn them of the destruction and expulsion that would come if they did not turn from their disobedience. Like a father giving 1, 2, 3, 4 warnings with increasing seriousness until no more warnings remain, God continually sent His servants to speak to His people.

> *Jeremiah 7:25-26 - "From the time your ancestors left Egypt until now,* ***day after day, again and again I [the LORD] sent you my servants the prophets.*** *But they did not listen to me or pay attention. They were stiff-necked and did more evil than their ancestors." (See also Jeremiah 25:4, 26:12-13, 44:4, and all the books of the Prophets.)*

Moreover, God's Prophets clearly spelled out exactly what the behaviors were that people needed to repent of and stop doing so that disaster would not come upon them. From many and various Scriptures throughout the writings of the Prophets, this list of oys or woes includes: accumulation of wealth and property for

17

luxurious living and feeling at ease; drunkenness and wild partying; saying that evil things are acceptable and calling righteous things evil; sexual immorality, promiscuity, and adultery; using deceptive trading tactics, greed, and usury for selfish gain; perverting justice particularly through bribery; forming alliances with people or nations and trusting in money or the strength of armies rather than trusting God; dishonoring parents and being wise in your own sight; mocking God and thinking that God cannot see or will not intervene against wickedness; taking vengeance against others through anger, wrath, and violence; singing songs and praying empty words to God without sincerity; living without grief at the state of the world; seeking the counsel of pagan spiritual leaders or false gods rather than seeking God and His ways in the Torah; having spiritual leaders, rabbis, teachers, prophets who lead people astray in the name of the LORD; and using service to the LORD or philanthropy as a means for personal gain or building a favorable reputation. (Study Isaiah 5, 30, Amos 4, 6, Habakkuk 2, Jeremiah 22-23, Ezekiel 13, 22, 34, and other passages.) Needless to say, this list covers much more than the rabbinic response of "idolatry."

But time and again, the Jewish people refused to listen. They preferred to listen to people claiming to be prophets, rabbis, and Torah scribes who said that because the Jewish people were chosen by God, destruction would never come to them or to God's Temple. (See Jeremiah 7 and 23; Micah 2 and 3, and other passages throughout the Prophets about false prophets and unfit leaders.) The people preferred to keep living their lives the way that they saw fit rather than return to the LORD and to the Torah.

Therefore, when the "sin thermometer" of the Jewish people became full and their collective and accumulated violations of the Torah warranted God's disciplinary action, God raised up adversaries to His own people. God used Gentile nations to inflict disciplinary blows upon His people—both the righteous and the wicked. (See Ezekiel 21:8-9.) Just as God sovereignly removed the protection over Gentile nations, He sovereignly removed His protection from the Jewish people.

*Isaiah 22:8 - **The Lord stripped away the defenses of Judah**, and you looked in that day to the weapons in the Palace of the Forest [man-made alliances and weaponry.]*

Israel, the northern kingdom of the Jewish people, blended in with the practices of the nations and sinned against God to a level which justly warranted judgment. They also failed to listen to numerous warnings and calls to repentance from God's Prophets. Consequently, God raised up the King of Assyria to conquer them and send them into exile. The Assyrians considered it to be a holy war as they conquered the people of Israel by the strength of their god, not knowing that they were only able to conquer because the God of Israel enabled them. (See 2 Chronicles 32:10-15.) The Assyrians were also known for being excessively violent and cruel in their torture of their enemies. Their conquests and deportations of Jews started in the year 742 BCE and ended in the year 722 BCE when the Assyrians had completely driven the Jewish people out of their land. Once the Jews had been removed, the Assyrians promptly set up their own religious monuments and settled their own religious leaders in the Land.

*2 Kings 17:6-9a, 13-15 - In the ninth year of Hoshea, **the king of Assyria captured Samaria and deported the Israelites to Assyria**. He settled them in Halah, in Gozan on the Habor River and in the towns of the Medes. **All this took place because the Israelites had sinned against the LORD their God**, who had brought them up out of Egypt from under the power of Pharaoh king of Egypt. They worshiped other gods and followed the practices of the nations the LORD had driven out before them, as well as the practices that the kings of Israel had introduced. **The Israelites secretly did things against the LORD their God that were not right**. ... **The LORD warned Israel and Judah through all his prophets and seers: "Turn from your evil ways**. Observe my commands and decrees, in accordance with the entire Law that I commanded your ancestors to obey and that I delivered to you through my servants the prophets." **But they would not listen and were as stiff-necked as their ancestors, who did not trust in the LORD their God. They rejected his decrees and the covenant he had made with their ancestors and the statutes he had warned them to keep**. They followed worthless idols and themselves became worthless. **They imitated the nations around them although the LORD had ordered them, "Do not do as they do."***

*1 Chronicles 5:26 - **So the God of Israel stirred up the spirit of Pul king of Assyria** (that is, Tiglath-Pileser king of Assyria), **who took the Reubenites, the Gadites and the half-tribe of Manasseh into exile.***

*2 Kings 18:11-12 - **The king of Assyria deported Israel to Assyria** and settled them in Halah, in Gozan on the Habor River and in towns of the Medes. **This happened because they had not obeyed the LORD their God, but had violated his covenant--**all that Moses the servant of the LORD commanded. They neither listened to the commands nor carried them out.*

Similarly, Judah, the southern kingdom of the Jewish people, even though they had seen the destruction of the northern kingdom, became worse than the northern kingdom in their wickedness. Their behavior was even more sinful than the pagan nations around them. The people of Judah also refused to repent in spite of the warnings of God's Prophets. So, God raised up Nebuchadnezzar to attack Jerusalem, capture the city, destroy the Temple, and expel the Jewish people from the Land. Jerusalem was sieged by Nebuchadnezzar in 597 BCE. Nebuchadnezzar also believed that he was being led by his gods and sought them for guidance, not knowing that it was the Most High God who was directing his steps. (See Ezekiel 21:21.) In fact, God gave Nebuchadnezzar great power to rule the whole world during his day. (See Jeremiah 27:1-8.) Nebuchadnezzar was also the ultimate demonstration of Babylon's cultural norms. The Babylonians were bent on self-sufficiency and making a name for themselves, obsessed with wealth and luxurious living, and were a people of unfair dealings in merchandise and trade for the sake of personal gain and advancement. Nebuchadnezzar's tactics against the people of Judah were merciless. Cities were plundered, babies and children were slaughtered, and no regard was given for the elderly. Women were raped, and men were tortured and put to death. Deportations of the Jewish people to Babylon were finalized in 586 BCE when the First Temple in Jerusalem was destroyed on the 9th of Av. Those who were not exiled were destroyed by violence, famines, plagues, and "natural disasters." This conquest was the Jewish holocaust of its day.

*Habakkuk 1:6-7 - **I [the LORD] am raising up the Babylonians,** that ruthless and impetuous people, **who sweep across the whole earth to seize dwellings not their own.** They are a feared and dreaded people; they are a law to themselves and promote their own honor.*

*Jeremiah 32:28-29 - Therefore this is what the LORD says: "**I am about to give this city into the hands of the Babylonians and to Nebuchadnezzar king of Babylon, who will capture it. The Babylonians who are attacking this city will come in and set it on fire; they will burn it down, along with the houses** where the people aroused my anger by burning incense on the roofs to Baal and by pouring out drink offerings to other gods."*

*Jeremiah 5:15-19 – "People of Israel," declares the LORD, "**I am bringing a distant nation [Babylon]*** *against you*--*an ancient and enduring nation, a people whose language you do not know, whose speech you do not understand.* **Their quivers are like an open grave; all of them are mighty warriors. They will devour your harvests and food, devour your sons and daughters; they will devour your flocks and herds, devour your vines and fig trees. With the sword they will destroy the fortified cities in which you trust**. *Yet even in those days,"* declares the LORD, *"I will not destroy you completely.* **And when the people ask, 'Why has the LORD our God done all this to us?' you will tell them, 'As you have forsaken me and served foreign gods in your own land, so now you will serve foreigners in a land not your own.'"**

Jeremiah 21:4-7 - This is what the LORD, the God of Israel, says: **"I am about to turn against you the weapons of war that are in your hands, which you are using to fight the king of Babylon and the Babylonians who are outside the wall besieging you**. *And I will gather them inside this city. I myself will fight against you with an outstretched hand and a mighty arm in furious anger and in great wrath.* **I will strike down those who live in this city--both man and beast--and they will die of a terrible plague**. *After that, declares the LORD, I will give Zedekiah king of Judah, his officials and* **the people in this city [Jerusalem] who survive the plague, sword and famine, into the hands of Nebuchadnezzar king of Babylon and to their enemies who want to kill them**. *He will put them to* *the sword;* **he will show them no mercy or pity or compassion.**"

It seemed completely nonsensical that God would work with Gentile nations who had no covenant with Him. It was contemptible to the Jewish way of thinking that God would use impure, violent, sinful, promiscuous people who worshipped wrong gods as a chastising tool against His own beloved covenant people. These Gentile nations were guilty of all of the offenses against God that we have listed for the Amorites. The Assyrians worshipped the wrong god, and God had previously judged the people of Babylon for their arrogance and narcissism in the Tower of Babel incident by scattering them to the four corners of the earth. (See Genesis 11.) But now, God was using these self-centered savages to conquer His own beloved people and the rest of the world. (Consider the Book of Habakkuk.)

This means that the suffering of the Jews was not the suffering of the righteous at the hands of angry Gentile nations, but was suffering as a consequence for their own sins. This was God's fatherly discipline for His beloved people.

I am certainly not condoning the evil behavior of the Gentiles who have persecuted and slaughtered the Jewish people. It was clearly evil. However, it is important to consider that God is Sovereign over all world events and could have put a halt to any of these types of persecutions and devastations throughout all of the centuries of Jewish history—but did not. And this was not only because of the evil in the Gentiles. Selah.

*Amos 3:6b - **When disaster comes to a city, has not the LORD caused it?***

*Isaiah 1:4, 9 - **Woe to the sinful nation [Israel], a people whose guilt is great, a brood of evildoers, children given to corruption! They have forsaken the LORD; they have spurned the Holy One of Israel and turned their backs on him. ... Unless the LORD Almighty had left us some survivors, we would have become like Sodom, we would have been like Gomorrah.***

Moreover, it is also significant to recognize God's mercy in the midst of judgment. Even though God Himself raised up Assyria and Babylon to conquer and scatter the Jewish people, destroy their cities, and demolish His Temple, God never allowed His chosen people to be completely destroyed like Sodom and Gomorrah, even though their sins merited it.

For God's Namesake

One person in the Bible who demonstrated understanding of this fact is Daniel. While in exile in Babylon, Daniel prayed to God on behalf of the Jewish people. His plea for mercy was not because the Jews had been unfairly and mercilessly treated by ruthless Gentile enemies as though they were righteous and did not deserve it. Daniel knew that it was God who had allowed adversaries to crush His own people and that by doing so He was being totally fair, faithful, and true to what He had said in the Torah.

Daniel 9:4-19 - I prayed to the LORD my God and confessed: "Lord, the great and awesome God, who keeps his covenant of love with those who love him and keep his commandments, we have sinned and done wrong. **We have been wicked and have rebelled; we have turned away from your commands and laws. We have not listened to your servants the prophets**, who spoke in your name to our kings, our princes and our ancestors, and to all the people of the land. **Lord, you are righteous, but this day we are covered with shame--the people of Judah and the inhabitants of Jerusalem and all Israel, both near and far, in all the countries where you have scattered us because of our unfaithfulness to you**. We and our kings, our princes and our ancestors are covered with shame, LORD, because we have sinned against you. The Lord our God is merciful and forgiving, even though we have rebelled against him; we have not obeyed the LORD our God or kept the laws he gave us through his servants the prophets. **All Israel has transgressed your law and turned away, refusing to obey you. Therefore the curses and sworn judgments written in the Law of Moses, the servant of God, have been poured out on us, because we have sinned against you. You have fulfilled the words spoken against us and against our rulers by bringing on us great disaster**. Under the whole heaven nothing has ever been done like what has been done to Jerusalem. **Just as it is written in the Law of Moses, all this disaster has come on us,** yet we have not sought the favor of the LORD our God by turning from our sins and giving attention to your truth. **The LORD did not hesitate to bring the** *disaster on us, for the LORD our God is righteous in everything he does; yet we have not obeyed him. Now, Lord our God, who brought your people out of Egypt with a mighty hand and **who made for yourself a name that endures to this day**, we have sinned, we have done wrong. Lord, in keeping with all your righteous acts, turn away your anger and your wrath from Jerusalem, your city, your holy hill. **Our sins and the iniquities of our ancestors have made Jerusalem and your people an object of scorn to all those around us.** Now, our God, hear the prayers and petitions of your servant. **For your sake, Lord, look with favor on your desolate sanctuary.** Give ear, our God, and hear; open your eyes and see the desolation of the city that bears your Name. **We do not make requests of you because we are righteous, but because of your great mercy.** Lord, listen! Lord, forgive! Lord, hear and act! **For your sake, my God, do not delay, because your city and your people bear your Name."***

All of this is to say that in spite of the waywardness of the Jewish people, God has never allowed the Jewish people to be completely destroyed—and He never will. Why? Because ever since God brought Israel out of Egypt through the parted waters of the Red Sea, the whole world knows that you are the chosen people of the Most High God. He is your God—and everybody in the world knows it.

The Jewish people exist to reveal God: His holiness, His power, and His ways. God has to execute judgment against the sins of the Jewish people, particularly when they blend into the ways of this world, or His righteousness and justice is not revealed. God has to preserve a remnant of His people in accordance with His promises to Abraham, or His faithfulness is not revealed. God has to bless the Jewish people with undeserved blessing, or else His mercy and goodness are not revealed.

Isaiah 48:10-11 - "See, I have refined you, though not as silver; ***I have tested you in the furnace of affliction. For my own sake, for my own sake, I do this. How can I let myself be defamed? I will not yield my glory to another. "*** *(See also Ezekiel 20.)*

The existence of the Jewish people proves the existence of their God—the only God who is Creator of the Universe. But more than that, the Jewish people are supposed to be an example for the world of God's righteousness and justice.

Think of it this way: If a highway has no speed limit, it is not against the law to speed. But if a highway does have a speed limit, then any driver driving at a speed exceeding the speed limit is breaking the law. Gentile nations do not have any law or speed limit from God and so, some drive too fast, others too slow, and they hardly know the purpose of different lanes and lines on the road. Jews, however, through the Torah, do have a law or speed limit which was designed to enable them to set the proper pace and demonstrate good driving habits for all the drivers in the world. When the Jewish people drive too fast or slow, or drive in reckless ways which endanger or harm other drivers, they are violating the law. Moreover, the legal consequences for speeding and bad driving have been clearly put forth in writing. If God does not punish Jewish driving, then the world will see Him as a weak law enforcer or think that He condones reckless driving even though it violates what He commanded. If God completely destroys the Jews for being poor drivers, then the world will consider Him to be an overzealous autocrat or a liar who does not keep His promises to their ancestors.

> *Isaiah 26:9b-10 - **When your judgments come upon the earth, the people of the world learn righteousness.** But when grace is shown to the wicked, they do not learn righteousness; even in a land of uprightness they go on doing evil and do not regard the majesty of the LORD.*

Therefore, God must execute justice *and* keep all of His promises to the Jewish people for all eternity for His own namesake. This also means that He has and will continue to preserve Israel forever so that His justice, absolute power, and Sovereignty over all nations is revealed to the whole world.

> *Ezekiel 36:22-23 - Therefore say to the Israelites, "This is what the Sovereign LORD says: '**It is not for your sake**, people of Israel, that I am going to do these things, but **for the sake of my holy name**, which you have profaned among the nations where you have gone. **I will show the holiness of my great name**, which has been profaned among the nations, the name you have profaned among them. **Then the nations will know that I am the LORD, declares the Sovereign LORD, when I am proved holy through***

you before their eyes.'"

Moses deeply understood that God would deal with His people for His namesake and pleaded with God on these grounds when God was ready to eliminate all the Israelites in the wilderness. Moses also prophesied from the beginning about Israel's wayward wanderings away from God and the Torah, the calamities that would come upon them as a consequence, and the reason why God will never allow the Jewish people to be fully extinguished.

*Numbers 14:13-18 - Moses said to the LORD, **"Then the Egyptians will hear about it!** By your power you brought these people up from among them. **And they will tell the inhabitants of this land about it. They have already heard that you, LORD, are with these people** and that you, LORD, have been seen face to face, that your cloud stays over them, and that you go before them in a pillar of cloud by day and a pillar of fire by night. **If you put all these people to death, leaving none alive, the nations who have heard this report about you will say, 'The LORD was not able to bring these people into the land he promised them on oath, so he slaughtered them in the wilderness.'** Now may the Lord's strength be displayed, just as you have declared: 'The LORD is slow to anger, abounding in love and forgiving sin and rebellion. Yet he does not leave the guilty unpunished; he punishes the children for the sin of the parents to the third and fourth generation.'" (See also Exodus 32.)*

Deuteronomy 32:26-27 - "I [the LORD] said I would

*scatter them [Jewish people] and erase their name from human memory, but I dreaded the taunt of the enemy, **lest the adversary misunderstand and say, 'Our hand has triumphed; the LORD has not done all this.'"***

No enemy of God or the Jewish people in heaven or earth or under the earth will ever be able to say that the God of Israel has had wicked intent for His people or was too weak to defend and preserve them. (I recommend reading Deuteronomy 4 and 32 and Ezekiel 20 in their entirety.)

Warnings to Flee and Return to the Land

One of the ways that God preserves His people for His namesake is through warnings of what is coming through His servants the Prophets. For example, while the Jewish people were in exile, God's Prophets were already prophesying about the destruction of the enemies of the Jews, particularly the Babylonian world empire which was doomed for destruction in the style of Sodom and Gomorrah.

*Isaiah 13:17-19 - "See, **I will stir up against them [the Babylonians] the Medes [the Persians], who do not care for silver and have no delight in gold [they are not in it for the money.]** Their bows will strike down the young men; they will have no mercy on infants, nor will they look with compassion on children. **Babylon, the jewel of kingdoms, the pride and glory of the Babylonians, will be overthrown by God like Sodom and Gomorrah."***

Like a chastising Father who articulates the exact

duration of punishment before it begins, God had explicitly stated through the Prophet Jeremiah that Jewish exile in Babylon would last for seventy years. During the time of exile, God encouraged His people to live life as usual in the land of their captivity and to pray for and bless the cities they inhabited. (See Jeremiah 29.) But after the seventy years of exile was completed, God had already issued a warning to His people to GET OUT of Babylon and to remember that their rightful home is in Jerusalem, the Promised Land.

*Jeremiah 51:44b-47 - And the wall of **Babylon will fall. "Come out of her, my people! Run for your lives! Run from the fierce anger of the LORD**. Do not lose heart or be afraid when rumors are heard in the land; one rumor comes this year, another the next, rumors of violence in the land and of ruler against ruler. **For the time will surely come when I will punish the idols of Babylon; her whole land will be disgraced and her slain will all lie fallen within her."***

*Jeremiah 51:49-50 NLT - "Just as Babylon killed the people of Israel and others throughout the world, so must her people be killed. **Get out, all you who have escaped the sword! Do not stand and watch--flee while you can!** Remember the LORD, though you are in a far-off land, and think about your home in Jerusalem."*

God's unwavering promise to Abraham would prove true. Those who bless Abraham and his descendants would be blessed and those who curse him and his people would be cursed. God promised that He would bring destruction to the nations who treat His people shamefully.

> *Jeremiah 46:27-28 - "Do not be afraid, Jacob my servant; do not be dismayed, Israel.* ***I will surely save you out of a distant place, your descendants from the land of their exile. Jacob will again have peace and security, and no one will make him afraid.*** *Do not be afraid, Jacob my servant, for I am with you," declares the LORD.* ***"Though I completely destroy all the nations among which I scatter you, I will not completely destroy you. I will discipline you but only in due measure; I will not let you go entirely unpunished."***

History proves that destruction did come to these nations exactly as God had said. God had warned His people to GET OUT of Babylon because He knew the time of Babylon's demise. The Jewish people who paid attention to the warnings from God's Prophets were not in Babylon when destruction came.

Gentile Nations Destroyed

As a consequence for their own wickedness and for inflicting blows upon the kingdoms of Israel, Assyria was overthrown by Babylon and a few generations later, Babylon was demolished by the Persians. All of this was in accordance with what was spoken by God's Prophets. God was again orchestrating international affairs to institute justice in the earth. The penalty for the sins of the Assyrians and Babylonians in addition to their treatment of the Jewish people merited their absolute termination.

Isaiah 10:5-6, 12 - **"Woe to the Assyrian, the rod of my anger, in whose hand is the club of my wrath! I send him against a godless nation [Israel], I dispatch him against a people who anger me, to seize loot and snatch plunder, and to trample them down like mud in the streets."...** *When the Lord has finished all his work against Mount Zion and Jerusalem, he will say,* **"I will punish the king of Assyria for the willful pride of his heart and the haughty look in his eyes.**

Jeremiah 50:9-11, 17-18 - "For **I will stir up and bring against Babylon an alliance of great nations from the land of the north.** *They will take up their positions against her, and from the north she will be captured. Their arrows will be like skilled warriors who do not return empty-handed. So* **Babylonia will be plundered;** *all who plunder her will have their fill," declares the LORD.* **"Because you rejoice and are glad, you who pillage my inheritance [Israel/the Jewish people]**, *because you frolic like a heifer threshing grain and neigh like stallions," ... "Israel is a scattered flock that lions have chased away. The first to devour them was the king of Assyria; the last to crush their bones was Nebuchadnezzar king of Babylon." Therefore this is what the LORD Almighty, the God of Israel, says:* **"I will punish the king of Babylon and his land as I punished the king of Assyria."**

Jeremiah 51:1-2 - This is what the LORD says: "See, **I will stir up the spirit of a destroyer against Babylon and the people of Leb Kamai. I will send**

34

foreigners to Babylon to winnow her and to devastate her land; they will oppose her on every side in the day of her disaster."

Furthermore, it is worth mentioning that there were nations surrounding the Promised Land who had attacked the Jewish people in their time of weakness, had been unhelpful to them, or had mocked them in their calamity. These nations also suffered the consequences for being unsupportive of the Jewish people. There are many passages in God's Prophets pertaining to these types of consequences, but consider particularly Ezekiel 25 and Amos 1-2. Needless to say, there are no Moabites, Edomites, or Philistines remaining in the world today.

Relevance for Today

This might and probably does reframe your outlook on international affairs and Who is really in charge. I'll stop there because all of these events are a matter of historical fact and by reviewing this history through the lens of Scripture, we have gained a reasonable level of Biblical understanding of God's dealings with nations, world powers, and the Jewish people.

Now it is time to return to today.

As we said before, King Solomon observed that what happened before will happen again. In addition to this, according to the great Torah scholars, there are four different and acceptable ways of interpreting Scripture. The first acceptable way of interpreting Scripture is called *pashat* which means a literal interpretation. Reading a passage this way is for the purpose of understanding what was literally happening as a historical event or what is literally being prophesied by God's Prophets that either has already or will in the future literally take place. The second acceptable way of interpreting Scripture is called *remez* which means hint or allusion. Reading a passage this way is a matter of understanding the things that God is alluding to or hinting at even though it may not be what is literally happening in the passage. These hints and allusions are an indication of some Scriptural theme or future or past event that God is deliberately alluding to or calling to mind, even though it is not the subject matter of the passage.

Furthermore, the Scriptures prophesy repeatedly about the great and terrible Day of the LORD which is still yet to come upon the inhabitants of the whole world. (This is only a sampling of Scriptures about the Day of the LORD.)

Isaiah 13:9-11 - See, **the day of the LORD is coming --a cruel day, with wrath and fierce anger-- to make the land desolate and destroy the sinners within it.** *The stars of heaven and their constellations will not show their light. The rising sun will be darkened and the moon will not give its light.* **I will punish the world for its evil, the wicked for their sins. I will put an end to the arrogance of the haughty and will humble the pride of the ruthless."*

Zephaniah 1:14-18 - **The great day of the LORD is near--near and coming quickly.** *The cry on the day of the LORD is bitter; the Mighty Warrior shouts his* battle cry. **That day will be a day of wrath--a day of distress and anguish, a day of trouble and ruin, a day of darkness and gloom, a day of clouds and blackness--a day of trumpet and battle cry against the fortified cities and against the corner towers. I will bring such distress on all people that they will grope about like those who are blind, because they have sinned against the LORD. Their blood will be poured out like dust and their entrails like dung. Neither their silver nor their gold will be able to save them on the day of the LORD's wrath. In the fire of his jealousy the whole earth will be consumed, for he will make a sudden end of all who live on the earth.**"

Amos 5:18-20 - **Woe to you who long for the day of the LORD!** *Why do you long for the day of the LORD?* **That day will be darkness, not light. It will be as though a man fled from a lion only to meet a bear, as though he entered his house and rested his hand on the wall only to have a snake bite him. Will not the day of the LORD be darkness, not light--pitch-dark, without a ray of brightness**?"

Joel 2:31-32 - **The sun will be turned to darkness [eclipse] and the moon to blood [blood moon] before the coming of the great and dreadful day of the LORD**. *And everyone who calls on the name of the LORD will be saved; for on Mount Zion and in Jerusalem there will be deliverance, as the LORD has said, even among the survivors whom the LORD calls.*

There have been many days in the course of history

which have seemed to fulfill many aspects of what is described by God's Prophets as the Day of the LORD. But those days were not the total fulfillment of it, as evidenced by the fact that we are all still here in this world. This means that historical events can also be a *remez* or hint or allusion pointing us to consider what is to come which will be even greater in severity of worldwide violence and devastation.

Accordingly, the events we have covered from the Scriptures and history have given us a strong indication of how God handles international affairs. God is not fickle. He has not changed His ways or His Torah. This means that we can safely conclude that the things which merited God's righteous judgment in the past are the same things that will merit God's intervention in international affairs today. God's interventions against the wickedness of Sodom and Gomorrah, the sin of the Amorites, the oppressive regime of the Egyptians, the erroneous religious zealousness of the Assyrians, and the arrogance and hedonism of the Babylonians in addition to His judgment of the whole earth in the days of Noah and against the pride of humanity in the days of the Tower of Babel are a mirror image of international catastrophes throughout history and give us an indication of the Day of the LORD to come.

Moreover, consider that it is a matter of historical fact that world empires have typically started out with strict codes of conduct for moral purity but have subsequently declined morally and spiritually before ultimately being scattered, conquered, and made to cease to exist. Some are more like Egypt, communism, Nazism, socialism, etc. and start off with intent to help the common man but eventually go the way of tyrannical rule, violence, oppression, and forced conformity of the common people. Others are more like Babylon, the Greek and Roman Empires, democracy, or the "westernized" world today, etc. and start off with intent to empower the common man but eventually degrade into lawlessness, materialism, sexual permissiveness, and hedonism. Some are more like Assyria or religiously zealous nations in that they consider that they are engaged in holy war and feel totally justified as servants of their god in attacking or condemning nations which promote or enable sin and impurity. Mixed into all of this are those who disregard God by means of intellectualism, atheism, pagan worship like the Amorites and pagans in the Promised Land before they were expelled. Or like the kingdoms of the Jewish people, there are those who approach worshipping the one true God in a way which has been watered down or secularized in order to blend in with modern culture rather than adhere to what the Torah actually says.

Do you see any of these types of things taking place in your nation? They most certainly are going on. All of these practices exhibit open-faced rebellion against the God who created the Universe and it is these things which will eventually fill up the "sin thermometer" of any nation. If any of these things are happening in your nation then, be assured—judgment and destruction are coming—and probably sooner than you think. Egypt, Assyria, and Babylon were all the most powerful regimes in the world in their day. People thought that they could never be destroyed. But God told His people everything that was going to happen because He knew the time of their demise and destruction.

If you are wise, you will be able to observe and discern the signs of the times. The last century has included more wars and violence than in any other century in history. The last century has included a great surge of hedonism and sexual permissiveness. The last century has included greater atrocities against the Jewish people than the Spanish Inquisition, the French and English expulsions, the Christian crusades, and the Russian pogroms. Anti-Semitism is ever-increasing. Like a woman in labor, all of these things are the birth pangs in the world, and they will only increase in severity and frequency in the days ahead.

As we stand today, God is about to judge the sin and wickedness of all of the nations in which you reside in a global conflict between world powers which will have characteristics resembling the traits of historical Egypt, Assyria, and Babylon. No one except God knows whether the "sin thermometer" of the world is filled enough to warrant the great and terrible Day of the LORD or if we have a few more rounds of warfare resembling this Day before it is fulfilled in its entirety. Regardless of this, we can be assured that these battles will not go well for you, your families, your businesses, or your life.

Fishers and Hunters

If you are Jewish, this means that it is time to return to

the Promised Land. Now is the time to GET OUT of the nations in which you reside. Your time of living in exile is complete. This is your warning: GO HOME. Let Jerusalem come to your mind. If you are Gentile, this means that it is time to seek the God of Israel and ask Him to have mercy on your soul. We will discuss this more in the next section of this book.

Although no Prophet foretold the length of time that the Jewish people would be exiled and scattered to the four corners of the earth, there are over seventy Scriptures that speak about the time when God's people will return to the Land promised to Abraham, Isaac, and Jacob. (A small selection of these Scriptures is supplied in the Appendix to this book.) For two thousand years this seemed utterly impossible, implausible, and highly unlikely. However, when the nation of Israel was established in 1948, God proved Himself holy in the sight of the nations by beginning to fulfill His promise to His people. Jews from around the world began to return to the Promised Land and call it their home. This return is called making Aliyah (ah-lee-ah.) These promises will only be fulfilled when not one Jew is left behind in any of the nations to which they have been scattered. Not one will be left behind.

*Deuteronomy 30:1-5 - When all these blessings and curses I have set before you come on you and you take them to heart **wherever the LORD your God disperses you among the nations**, and when you and your children return to the LORD your God and obey him with all your heart and with all your soul according to everything I command you today, **then***

the LORD your God will restore your fortunes and have compassion on you and gather you again from all the nations where he scattered you. Even if you have been banished to the most distant land under the heavens, from there the LORD your God will gather you and bring you back. He will bring you to the land that belonged to your ancestors, and you will take possession of it. *He will make you more prosperous and numerous than your ancestors.*

Isaiah 11:11-12, 16 - In that day the Lord **will reach out his hand a second time to reclaim the surviving remnant of his people from Assyria, from Lower Egypt, from Upper Egypt, from Cush, from Elam, from Babylonia, from Hamath and from the islands of the Mediterranean**. *He will raise a banner for the nations and gather the exiles of Israel;* **he will assemble the scattered people of Judah from the four quarters of the earth**. *...* **There will be a highway for the remnant of his people that is left from Assyria, as there was for Israel when they came up from Egypt**.

Isaiah 43:4-7 - "Since you are precious and honored in my sight, and because I love you, I will give people in exchange for you, nations in exchange for your life. Do not be afraid, for I am with you; ***I will bring your children from the east and gather you from the west. I will say to the north, 'Give them up!' and to the south, 'Do not hold them back.' Bring my sons from afar and my daughters from the ends of the earth--everyone who is called by my name, whom I created for my glory, whom I***

42

formed and made."

Jeremiah 23:7-8 - "So then, the days are coming,"
declares the LORD, "when people will no longer
say, 'As surely as the LORD lives, who brought the
*Israelites up out of Egypt,' but they will say, **'As***
surely as the LORD lives, who brought the
descendants of Israel up out of the land of the
north and out of all the countries where he had
banished them.' Then they will live in their own
land."

*Ezekiel 39:27-28 - "**When I have brought them***
back from the nations and have gathered them
***from the countries of their enemies**, I will be*
proved holy through them in the sight of many
nations. Then they will know that I am the LORD
*their God, **for though I sent them into exile among***
the nations, I will gather them to their own land,
***not leaving any behind**."*

The return of God's people to the Land of Israel after
two thousand years of exile is an even greater miracle
than parting the waters of the Red Sea to grant them
escape from Egypt. Moreover, it is God's expressed
purpose that not one Jewish person will be left out of
God's plan for His people. However, as the Scripture
says, God will fulfill His plan of gathering all of the
Jews out of the nations by first sending fishers and then
sending hunters.

Jeremiah 16:14-16 - "However, the days are
coming," declares the LORD, "when it will no
*longer be said, **'As surely as the LORD lives, who***

brought the Israelites up out of Egypt,' but it will be said, 'As surely as the LORD lives, who brought the Israelites up out of the land of the north and out of all the countries where he had banished them.' For I will restore them to the land I gave their ancestors. But now I will send for many fishermen," declares the LORD, "and they will catch them. After that I will send for many hunters, and they will hunt them down on every mountain and hill and from the crevices of the rocks."

Think of it this way, fishers use a net which gently drags the fish to the shore, preserving the life of the fish until they arrive safely in the harbor. Hunters however, hunt with intent to kill. Hunters do not care if you make it to the land alive or if you die after being chased out of the nation you are living in.

If you are Jewish then, you have a question to ask yourself: Would you rather be fished or hunted? If you prefer to be fished, then take this as your warning, leave the nation where you are living, and move to the Land of Israel. Don't waste time. The sooner the better. There are programs and many, many people who have devoted their lives to helping the Jewish people from all nations make Aliyah to Israel. (There is a small list of Aliyah resources in the Appendix of this book.) This help is also a fulfillment of Scripture that even Gentiles will help Jews return to the Promised Land.

Isaiah 14:1-2 - The LORD will have compassion on Jacob; once again he will choose Israel and will settle them in their own land. Foreigners will join them and unite with the descendants of Jacob.

Nations will take them and bring them to their own place. And Israel will take possession of the nations and make them male and female servants in the LORD's land. *They will make captives of their captors and rule over their oppressors.*

Yes, I know that starting again will have its challenges but there is no challenge greater than the horror of being hunted by the hunters that God will send to fetch you. God knows who you are and where you are. The hunters He sends to find you will not care if you are a faithful Jew or a wayward Jew. They will only care that you are a Jew. When the hunters come with their persecutions, pogroms, violence, and terror, Scripture compares this to the time when the entire Israelite generation had to die in the wilderness before He could bestow His blessings upon His people in the Land. Please don't die in the nation of your choosing because you did not heed this warning.

Ezekiel 20:33-38 - "As surely as I live," declares the Sovereign LORD, "I will reign over you with a mighty hand and an outstretched arm and with outpoured wrath. ***I will bring you from the nations and gather you from the countries where you have been scattered--with a mighty hand and an outstretched arm and with outpoured wrath. I will bring you into the wilderness of the nations and there, face to face, I will execute judgment upon you.*** *As I judged your ancestors in the wilderness of the land of Egypt, so I will judge you," declares the Sovereign LORD.* ***"I will take note of you as you pass under my rod, and I will bring you into the*** *bond of the covenant. I will purge you of those who revolt and rebel against me. Although I will bring them out of the land where they are living, yet they will not enter the land of Israel. Then you will know that I am the LORD."*

Zechariah 13:8-9 - "In the whole land," declares the LORD, "two-thirds will be struck down and perish; yet one-third will be left in it. This third I will put into the fire; I will refine them like silver and test them like gold. They will call on my name and I will answer them; I will say, 'They are my people,' and they will say, 'The LORD is our God.'"

I know that these passages are intense. But please be mindful that there are also examples in history which demonstrate God's seriousness in executing His plan to restore His chosen people to the Promised Land. It saddens me greatly to say it, but these passages were partially fulfilled through the horrific events of the Holocaust of World War II. As a *remez* or hint of the Day of the LORD to come, the Jews of Europe were unilaterally expelled from their dwelling places, plundered, exiled, and sent to horrifying labor camps where two thirds of the Jewish population in Europe was exterminated, as Zechariah prophesied. These events also immediately preceded the formation of the State of Israel for the Jews who survived the outpoured wrath and passed under the rod of God which Ezekiel prophesied. As grave and terrible as that time was, there is still a holocaust yet to come when these types of events take place on a global basis, expelling the Jewish people from every nation in the world. It is commonly

known as the time of *Jacob's Trouble* because of this
passage of Scripture:

*Jeremiah 30:1-24 - This is the word that came to
Jeremiah from the LORD: This is what the LORD,
the God of Israel, says: "Write in a book all the
words I have spoken to you. The days are coming,"
declares the LORD,* **"when I will bring my people
Israel and Judah back from captivity and restore
them to the land I gave their ancestors to possess**,"
*says the LORD. These are the words the LORD
spoke concerning Israel and Judah: This is what the
LORD says:* **"Cries of fear are heard--terror, not
peace. Ask and see: Can a man bear children?
Then why do I see every strong man with his hands
on his stomach like a woman in labor, every face
turned deathly pale? How awful that day will be!
No other will be like it. It will be a time of trouble
for Jacob, but he will be saved out of it**. *In that
day," declares the LORD Almighty,* **"I will break the
yoke off their necks and will tear off their bonds;
no longer will foreigners enslave them**. *Instead,
they will serve the LORD their God and David their
king, whom I will raise up for them. So do not be
afraid, Jacob my servant; do not be dismayed,
Israel," declares the LORD.* **"I will surely save you
out of a distant place, your descendants from the
land of their exile. Jacob will again have peace and
security, and no one will make him afraid.** *I am
with you and will save you," declares the LORD.
"Though I completely destroy all the nations among
which I scatter you, I will not completely destroy*

47

*you. I will discipline you but only in due measure; I will not let you go entirely unpunished." This is what the LORD says: "Your wound is incurable, your injury beyond healing. There is no one to plead your cause, no remedy for your sore, no healing for you. **All your allies have forgotten you; they care nothing for you.** I have struck you as an enemy would and punished you as would the cruel, because your guilt is so great and your sins so many. Why do you cry out over your wound, your pain that has no cure? Because of your great guilt and many sins I have done these things to you. But all who devour you will be devoured; all your enemies will go into exile. Those who plunder you will be plundered; all who make spoil of you I will despoil. **But I will restore you to health and heal your wounds,"** declares the LORD, "because you are called an outcast, Zion for whom no one cares." This is what the LORD says: **"I will restore the fortunes of Jacob's tents and have compassion on his dwellings; the city will be rebuilt on her ruins, and the palace will stand in its proper place. From them will come songs of thanksgiving and the sound of rejoicing. I will add to their numbers, and they will not be decreased; I will bring them honor, and they will not be disdained. Their children will be as in days of old, and their community will be established before me; I will punish all who oppress them.** Their leader will be one of their own; their ruler will arise from among them. I will bring him near and he will come close to me--for who is he who will devote himself to be close to me?" declares*

48

*the LORD. **"So you will be my people, and I will be your God."** See, **the storm of the LORD will burst out in wrath, a driving wind swirling down on the heads of the wicked. The fierce anger of the LORD will not turn back until he fully accomplishes the purposes of his heart. In days to come you will understand this***.

The holocaust still yet to come will be even worse than what has already occurred in history and will take place in all the nations of the earth. God will send hunters to hunt His people who have refused to be fished. Please, please, PLEASE consider this very seriously. Before the Holocaust of World War II, there were many warning signs and literal/verbal/written warnings from lovers of the Jewish people to urge them to leave the countries for safety. Most did not listen. If you are reading this book, consider yourself warned. Do not mock or scoff because these things were declared by God and will surely come to pass.

Blessings in the Promised Land

There is also good news for the Jewish people which will come to pass for you if you heed this warning to return to the Land. God's intent for you in the Promised Land is to BLESS you, ESTABLISH you, MULTIPLY you, and PROSPER you.

*Amos 9:14-15 - "...and I will bring my people Israel back from exile. **They will rebuild the ruined cities and live in them. They will plant vineyards and drink their wine; they will make gardens and eat their fruit. I will plant Israel in their own land,***

never again to be uprooted from the land I have given them," *says the LORD your God.*

Jeremiah 32:41-42 – "**I [the LORD] will rejoice in doing them good and will assuredly plant them in this land with all my heart and soul**." *This is what the LORD says:* "**As I have brought all this great calamity on this people, so I will give them all the prosperity I have promised them**."

Zechariah 8:7-15 - This is what the LORD Almighty says: "**I will save my people from the countries of the east and the west. I will bring them back to live in Jerusalem; they will be my people, and I will be faithful and righteous to them as their God.**" *This is what the LORD Almighty says:* "*Now hear these words,* **Let your hands be strong so that the temple may be built.** *This is also what the prophets said who were present when the foundation was laid for the house of the LORD Almighty. Before that time there were no wages for people or hire for animals. No one could go about their business safely because of their enemies, since I had turned everyone against their neighbor.* **But now I will not deal with the remnant of this people as I did in the past,**" *declares the LORD Almighty.* "**The seed will grow well, the vine will yield its fruit, the ground will produce its crops, and the heavens will drop their dew. I will give all these things as an inheritance to the remnant of this people**. *Just as you, Judah and Israel, have been a curse among the nations, so I will save you, and you will be a blessing. Do not be afraid, but let your hands be strong." This is what* the LORD Almighty says: **"Just as I had determined to bring disaster on you and showed no pity when your ancestors angered me," says the LORD Almighty, "so now I have determined to do good again to Jerusalem and Judah. Do not be afraid."**

Ezekiel 36:24-30, 34-35 - **"For I will take you out of the nations; I will gather you from all the countries and bring you back into your own land.** *I will sprinkle clean water on you, and you will be clean; I will cleanse you from all your impurities and from all your idols. I will give you a new heart and put a new spirit in you; I will remove from you your heart of stone and give you a heart of flesh. And I will put my Spirit in you and move you to follow my decrees and be careful to keep my laws.* **Then you will live in the land I gave your ancestors; you will be my people, and I will be your God.** *I will save you from all your uncleanness.* **I will call for the grain and make it plentiful and will not bring famine upon you. I will increase the fruit of the trees and the crops of the field, so that you will no longer suffer disgrace among the nations because of famine. ... The desolate land will be cultivated instead of lying desolate in the sight of all who pass through it. They will say, 'This land that was laid waste has become like the garden of Eden; the cities that were lying in ruins, desolate and destroyed, are now fortified and inhabited. '"**

Ezekiel 37:21-28 - and say to them, This is what the Sovereign LORD says: **"I will take the Israelites out of the nations where they have gone. I will gather**

them from all around and bring them back into their own land. I will make them one nation in the land, on the mountains of Israel. *There will be one king over all of them and they will never again be two nations or be divided into two kingdoms. They will no longer defile themselves with their idols and vile images or with any of their offenses, for I will save them from all their sinful backsliding, and I will cleanse them.* **They will be my people, and I will be their God.** *My servant David will be king over them, and they will all have one shepherd. They will follow my laws and be careful to keep my decrees.* **They will live in the land I gave to my servant Jacob, the land where your ancestors lived. They and their children and their children's children will live there forever**, *and David my servant will be their prince forever. I will make a covenant of peace with them; it will be an everlasting covenant.* **I will establish them and increase their numbers, and I will put my sanctuary among them forever. My dwelling place will be with them; I will be their God, and they will be my people. Then the nations will know that I the LORD make Israel holy, when my sanctuary is among them forever.**"

The time has come for God to bless you in the Land that He promised to your ancestors. Plus, if you noticed in the text of these Scriptures, He also promises to cleanse you of your unrighteousness. This means that if you have been participating in or ensnared by the cultural norms of materialism, drunkenness, sexual permissiveness, hedonism, violence, false spirituality and the other activities noted as the reasons why God allowed people and nations to be overrun, God will grant you mercy and will cleanse you of these offenses. We will discuss this more in the next section of this book.

The Day to Come

Moreover, the day will come when the Land of Israel is the only safe place in the world to be Jewish. In the final conflict, God will draw ALL the nations of the earth to the Valley of Jehoshaphat, which is the Kidron Valley in Jerusalem to the East of the Temple Mount and the City of David. God will enter into judgment with ALL nations the way that He judged Babylon, Assyria, the Egyptians, the Amorites, and Sodom and Gomorrah.

*Joel 3:1-2 - "In those days and at that time, when I restore the fortunes of Judah and Jerusalem, I **will gather all nations and bring them down to the Valley of Jehoshaphat. There I will put them on trial for what they did to my inheritance, my people Israel, because they scattered my people among the nations and divided up my land."***

In that day, Israel is the only place that you will want yourself and your family to be. Although God does not promise that living in Israel will be completely problem or conflict free, He does declare His protection to those who live in the Promised Land in the Day to come.

*Zechariah 12:2-9 - "**I am going to make Jerusalem a cup that sends all the surrounding peoples reeling. Judah will be besieged as well as Jerusalem. On that day, when all the nations of the earth are gathered against her, I will make***

Jerusalem an immovable rock for all the nations. All who try to move it will injure themselves. On that day I will strike every horse with panic and its rider with madness," declares the LORD. "*I will keep a watchful eye over Judah,* but I will blind all the horses of the nations. Then the clans of Judah will say in their hearts, 'The people of Jerusalem are strong, because the LORD Almighty is their God.' *On that day I will make the clans of Judah like a firepot in a woodpile, like a flaming torch among sheaves. They will consume all the surrounding peoples right and left, but Jerusalem will remain intact in her place.*" The LORD will save the dwellings of Judah first, so that the honor of the house of David and of Jerusalem's inhabitants may not be greater than that of Judah. *On that day the LORD will shield those who live in Jerusalem, so that the feeblest among them will be like David,* and the house of David will be like God, like the angel of the LORD going before them. *On that day I will set out to destroy all the nations that attack Jerusalem.*"

In that Day, where will you be? In that Day, who will you stand for? Will you be fighting alongside the God of Israel or be crushed as one of His enemies?

Whether you decide to try to remain in the nations or move voluntarily to the Land of Israel, there will be trials, wars, and calamities of every kind in the days ahead. All of creation and every nation is drawing ever nearer to the Day of the LORD and the fulfillment of all that is written. Not one word of God's Prophets will fail to come to pass in literal fulfillment of all that has been decreed. In the end, the God of Israel who is the only Creator of the Universe will stand victoriously above all the nations of the earth. He will judge the living and the dead in the resurrection of the just and the unjust. Some will go to everlasting life while others will be banished to everlasting shame and disgrace. (See Daniel 7, 12.)

Perhaps you will heed this warning and perhaps you will not. But consider this. Regardless of where you find yourself when calamity comes upon all the nations of the earth, it is time to think about who you are and what you are willing to die for. The day will come when you will have to give an account for whether you have been more concerned about those who can kill your body or if you have given regard to the God of Israel, the only One who is able to kill your soul.

2

THE WAR FOR YOUR SOUL

The war for your soul is an ancient war. It is a war between good and evil or light and darkness. It is a war between God, who is the giver of life, and His adversary, Satan, who does everything in his power to bring rebellion, destruction, and death.

From the birth of the Jewish people as a nation at Passover, when God brought you out of Egypt, God has had a unique purpose for you in this epic battle. God chose Israel to be a Kingdom of priests who would worship Him, bear His image of righteousness, rule over the powers of darkness, crush the evil one, and bless the whole world.

> *Exodus 19:5-6 - "Now if you obey me fully and keep my covenant, then **out of all nations you will be my treasured possession**. Although the whole earth is mine, **you will be for me a kingdom of priests and a holy nation**." These are the words you are to speak to the Israelites.*

God's purpose for Israel was never for Israel to be a nation like all the other nations of the earth. His purpose was not for you to be a superior people simply because you have Him as your God and He is a superior God—the only true God and the only Creator of the Universe. Rather, His design for you was to be a Kingdom for Him, like the Kingdom of Heaven on earth.

In the Beginning

Actually, God's plan for His Kingdom started long before He designated Israel as the people chosen to carry forth this destiny. Before the creation of this world and mankind, God's chief worship leader was an angel named Lucifer. But Lucifer desired to be like God and to sit on God's throne. Lucifer wanted to be worshipped and have authority over all things for himself. So he launched a rebellion against God which God speedily crushed. Lucifer was banished from Heaven along with the angels who had joined in his rebellion, and he became known as Satan, which means *the adversary* of God. (This occurred between Genesis 1:1 and Genesis 1:2 and is reflected in more detail in Isaiah 14 and Ezekiel 28.)

Soon after this rebellion when God spoke creation into existence, Satan was thrown down to the earth in the form of a serpent. God created mankind to rule over Satan. In the same way that in the first section of this book, we witnessed God orchestrating international affairs and granting authority to rule over and crush nations which were in rebellion against Him, God orchestrated eternal affairs to punish the rebellion of the adversary. This means that from the beginning of creation as we know it, God's purpose for mankind is to be a Kingdom of God on the earth, displaying His authority by ruling the earth in accordance with His ways and trampling the evil one. God created mankind to bear His image, have eternal life, and hold the keys to His Kingdom. (See Genesis 1-2.)

Unfortunately, Adam and Eve, who were made in God's likeness as His key-holding, world-ruling image-bearers, took the advice of the serpent whom they were supposed to rule over. They disobeyed God's instructions and displayed that they were more like the adversary than like God. In the interest of personal advancement through the knowledge of good and evil, they were drawn to rebellion against God even though it entailed risking death. Therefore, maintaining His Sovereignty in keeping with the consequences He had warned would result from their disobedience, Adam and Eve were banished from Eden. They lost the right to rule the earth with God, forfeited the eternal life which God had designed them for, and had the keys to the Kingdom of God taken from them. However, even in their punishment, God granted a ray of hope by promising that one of the woman's descendants, her seed, would crush the head of the serpent and re-possess the keys to the Kingdom of God for mankind. This promised descendant is who we have come to know as the Messiah—the Anointed One of God. (See Genesis 3.)

Was this calling fulfilled by one of their immediate sons? No. Adam and Eve's rebellion against God's ways very quickly became evident in their children. Their elder son Cain, in the likeness of the adversary rather than God, killed their younger son Abel because Cain was jealous that God accepted Abel's blood sacrifice as an offering but did not accept his bloodless offering. Even though he was the firstborn son and apparent rightful heir, Cain was consequently banished even further from Eden and driven from any hope of ruling the earth with God. (See Genesis 4.) As Adam and Eve had more children and the generations continued down the line, it became evident that every thought in the minds of Adam and Eve's descendants tended to evil all the time. (See Genesis 6:5.) Mankind continued to chose the ways of the adversary and displayed more of the adversary's likeness than God's.

A Remnant of One Man

Therefore, God started over again with a remnant of one, a man named Noah. In all the earth, God found only Noah to be blameless. God walked in relationship with Noah and instructed Noah to build an ark, a boat, which would house a remnant of creation. Once Noah and his family were safe, God maintained His sovereignty as Creator and judged the whole earth for its wickedness and rebellion against Him. A great flood filled the earth, killing and destroying everyone and everything that was not inside Noah's Ark. After the flood, God instructed Noah and his sons to fill the earth with descendants, and He granted them a small degree of restored Kingdom authority over creation. God also entered into a covenant with Noah, promising that He would never again destroy the earth by flood. (See Genesis 6-9.)

As generations continued to be born, mankind proved to have an innate determination to rebel against God just like Adam and Eve had. Instead of desiring to rule the earth as a Kingdom for and with God, they took rebellion to a whole new level and gathered together to build a kingdom for themselves. In the likeness of the adversary, they put their knowledge of good and evil to work and built the Tower of Babel to make a name for themselves. This tower was their symbol of self-empowerment and rejection of God altogether. So, God again maintained His rightful authority as God by scattering peoples to the ends of the earth and giving them different languages in order to impede any further rebellions of this sort. (See Genesis 11.)

At this point, God's Kingdom destiny for mankind as His image bearers in the earth seemed all but lost and hopeless.

One Chosen Man

Therefore, God again selected one man as a remnant to carry forth His Kingdom purposes for mankind. God chose Abraham. Out of all the peoples in all the earth, God chose one man to walk with Him. God entered into a covenant with Abraham which was sealed with the blood of sacrifices. God promised to bless Abraham with a land of his own and make Him into a nation of people—a Kingdom that would bless all the nations of the earth. The Messiah, the One who would crush the head of the serpent and establish the Kingdom of God on the earth, was now promised to come through one of Abraham's descendants. (See Genesis 12, 15.) Essentially, God exclusively transferred to Abraham the right to the keys to the Kingdom of God and the governing role originally bestowed to Adam and Eve.

Abraham believed God and this faith was credited to

him as righteousness. This means that even though Abraham's behavior was not always completely kosher, God did not hold Abraham's errors against him, nor did He hold the sins of Abraham's ancestors against him. Because of Abraham's faith, God treated him as if he had a perfect record of righteousness. Abraham's faith was also evidenced by his actions. He left everything he had ever known to follow God's call. He left his country, his father's household, and his father's traditions, and his ancestor's approach to religion and spiritual life. He set out looking to establish the Kingdom of God in the earth, no matter what it cost him. Even the Gentiles recognized Abraham as a prince among them. (See Genesis 23:6.)

Now that the Messiah was going to be born through Abraham, was it Abraham's immediate son who would bear God's image and trample the head of the adversary? No. Abraham and his wife Sarah waited a long time for an heir, even past the point of her menstruation and child-bearing years. Eventually, angels visited them and told them that they would have a son and they were to name him Isaac. Through a miraculous conception, Sarah became pregnant at age ninety after being barren her whole life. Abraham was one hundred years old when their son Isaac arrived.

After a while, God tested Abraham's faith to see if he was a worthy steward of the keys to the Kingdom. Would he falter as Adam and Eve had? God told Abraham to go to Mount Moriah and offer Isaac, his only son, as a sacrifice. According to any reasonable concept of good and evil, this makes no sense whatsoever. But Abraham trusted God as the source of life who was even able to raise Isaac from the dead to fulfill His promises. In trust, he set out to obey God's command rather than rebel against Him. Before Abraham was able to slay Isaac on top of Mount Moriah, an angel stopped him and pointed out that God provided a ram to be sacrificed instead. The angel also confirmed that Abraham, through his humble submission and faithfulness to God, had passed the test. Abraham had not taken matters into his own hands as Adam and Eve had. Now, most assuredly, the Messiah would come through Abraham's descendants to crush the head of the adversary and hold the keys to the Kingdom of God. Then, Abraham saw into the future and prophesied that on the same mountain, the Mountain of the Lord, God would see to the fulfillment of this promise. (See Genesis 22.)

God's covenant with Abraham was transferred exclusively to his son Isaac. Then, through another miraculous conception, Isaac and his wife Rebekah had twin sons Esau and Jacob. Esau was the elder and apparent heir. However, the birthright of inheriting the right to the keys to the Kingdom of God was foreordained by God to pass to Jacob, the younger brother. Long story short, through a series of events, Esau rejected his birthright and sold it to Jacob for a bowl of lentils. Therefore, God's covenant with Abraham transferred exclusively from Isaac to Jacob, whose name God later changed to Israel.

Jacob, later Israel, had twelve sons who had sons and daughters and became the twelve tribes of Israel. Jacob's favorite son, Joseph, had two dreams from God showing that the rest of his family was going to bow down to him and serve him. Jacob, as God's covenant carrier in his generation who knew the prophecies and promises given his fathers, took note of this. It is possible that Jacob considered that Joseph might be the promised Messiah who was going to be entrusted with the keys to the Kingdom of God. Joseph's brothers however, rejected Joseph's dreams entirely and threw him in a pit to leave him for dead before selling him to some Gentiles passing by. The Gentiles brought Joseph to Egypt to serve as a slave. After many years and a series of divinely orchestrated events, Joseph was appointed second in command to Pharaoh, the most powerful man in the world at that time. Pharaoh also changed Joseph's name to Zaphnath-Paaneah in order for him to seem less Hebrew and more Egyptian. (See Genesis 41:45.) Soon after this, Joseph's brothers came to Egypt to acquire food because there was famine in the land of Canaan where they were still living. After all the years that had passed and the changes that had taken place, Joseph's brothers did not recognize Joseph at first but considered him to be a leader of the Gentiles. But when they finally did recognize him as their brother, they were grieved at how they had treated him and asked for his forgiveness—a forgiveness he mercifully extended to them. Everything that God had revealed to Joseph came to pass. He had been granted great authority in the earth, and his brothers did bow down to him.

The God of Israel received great glory on a global basis during this time. Joseph had God-given wisdom and was a righteous image-bearer for God with no record of sin according to Scripture. When this was combined with Joseph's position of authority as second in command under Pharaoh who was the most powerful man in the world at that time, Joseph was responsible for feeding the whole world during a time of global famine. However, God had a different kind of Kingdom in mind for His people. He had a plan to bring forth image-bearers who were second to no one but Him, the way it had originally been in the Garden of Eden with Adam and Eve. Furthermore, even though Joseph was considered a prince among his brothers in his generation, when the time came for Jacob to bless his sons and pass the covenant promises of God to the next generation, Jacob prophesied that the scepter of God's Kingdom would be carried not through his son Joseph but through Judah. (See Genesis 49.)

A Chosen Nation and Kingdom of Priests

Later, after Jacob's descendants had multiplied through the course of several generations, God chose the whole nation of Israel for His purposes. God sent Moses to deliver them from Egyptian slavery exactly as and when He promised He would. God worked miracles for Moses as His servant so that the Jewish people would see the power of the Kingdom of Heaven follow Moses as His chosen servant. Finally, after nine plagues of judgment against the Egyptians and their false gods, Moses told Pharaoh that God was going to send the Destroyer to kill all the first born sons in Egypt. At the same time, Moses told the Israelites to slaughter a lamb for each household and paint the lamb's blood on the doorpost of their homes. When God saw the blood on the doorposts, He would *pass over* the house and not allow the Destroyer to enter. Instead of death, God now required His people to dedicate to Him every firstborn male as a priest of God. This would mean that almost every Jewish household would have a priest in it to keep the ways of God constantly before all of His people. (See Exodus 1-13.)

After their deliverance from Egypt, God instructed the Israelites to wash and ceremonially cleanse themselves so that He could enter into covenant with them. At Sinai, God's power appeared in an all-consuming fire over the Mount, and there the Israelites were afraid of God. They recognized that God was too holy for them to approach on their own. They saw that they would die if they entered God's presence or spoke to Him directly. Therefore, they requested that Moses be the Mediator between them and God, and God granted their request. From this point forward, according to the law, the Jewish people could not approach God directly but required a Mediator to stand between them and God. In their generation, it was Moses, but Moses promised that in keeping with Israel's need for a Mediator, God would appoint a Prophet like Moses, the Messiah, who would speak the words of God and be the One to whom Israel must listen even more closely than they did Moses. (See Exodus 20, Deuteronomy 5, 18.)

It was at Sinai that God gave His people the Torah and entered into covenant with Israel which was sealed with the blood of sacrifices. (See Exodus 19-24.) The Torah instituted the Ten Commandments and other rules and regulations which God commanded the Israelites to keep and obey. The Torah also established the Tabernacle of God as the predecessor to the Temple and God's sacrificial system by which Israel could atone for their sins through blood sacrifices. When individuals or the collective community of Israel rebelled against God in the likeness of Adam and Eve or committed violations of the Torah, either knowingly or unintentionally, the Torah system requires the shedding of the blood of an unblemished sacrifice to atone for their sins. The Torah commands that at God's designated place for sacrifice, the sins of the people must be confessed as they lay their hands upon a spotless sacrificial lamb, transferring their sins to the lamb. Then, the lamb is slaughtered, shedding its blood as atonement and dying the death penalty in the place of the person who had committed error. According to the Torah, only blood can make atonement for the soul. Without the shedding of blood, there is no atonement. (It is for this reason that Jewish people do not eat blood and why kosher butchers drain blood the way that they do to this day.)

Leviticus 17:11-12 NKJV - ***"For the life of the flesh is in the blood, and I have given it to you upon the altar to make atonement for your souls; for it is the blood that makes atonement for the soul.***" *Therefore I said to the children of Israel, "No one among you shall eat blood, nor shall any stranger who dwells among you eat blood."*

Through obedience to the Torah, God had granted the keys to His Kingdom, to righteousness, and to eternal life exclusively to Israel out of all the peoples of the earth.

> *Leviticus 18:5 - "**Keep my decrees and laws, for the person who obeys them will live [have eternal life] by them**. I am the LORD." (See also Deuteronomy 4:1, 40, 5:33, 8:1, 16:20, 30:16, 19.)*

> *Deuteronomy 6:24-25 - **The LORD commanded us to obey** all these decrees and to fear the LORD our God, **so that we might always prosper and be kept alive [have eternal life],** as is the case today. **And if we are careful to obey all this law [Torah]** before the LORD our God, as he has commanded us, **that will be our righteousness**.*

If Israel listened to God and obeyed the Torah, they would be His royal Kingdom people and would rule the earth because God would raise them high above all other nations. Moreover, by walking in God's ways according to the Torah, Israel would fulfill their destiny as God's Kingdom of image-bearers, displaying His wisdom, righteousness, and holiness as a blessing to all the earth.

> *Deuteronomy 4:6 - **Observe them carefully, for this will show your wisdom and understanding to the nations,** who will hear about all these decrees and say, "Surely this great nation is a wise and understanding people."*

On the other hand, if Israel went the way of Adam and Eve, displaying the likeness of God's adversary through disobedience to the Torah, then there would be consequences. In fact, the Torah specifically outlines the blessings for obedience and curses for disobedience, as we discussed a bit in the last section of this book. (See

Leviticus 26; Deuteronomy 28.) That said, in spite of disobedience to the Torah given through Moses, God will never completely abandon Israel because of His everlasting one-sided covenant promises to Abraham, Isaac, and Jacob.

A New Generation

Unfortunately, the Israelites in the wilderness repeatedly rebelled against Moses and they constantly questioned his authority as God's only appointed leader and Mediator. They rejected God and worshipped a Golden Calf as the being who had brought them out of Egypt. They grumbled and despised the wilderness God had placed them in, and they tried on several occasions to appoint leaders for themselves who would meet their demands to return to Egypt, even though they had been slaves there. As the consequence for such insolence, God was ready to destroy the Israelites and start all over again with a remnant of one man, Moses. But Moses prayed to God on Israel's behalf, and God did not destroy them and start over. It was at this time that the Levites proved faithful to God, siding with Moses and the Lord. The Levites were even willing to slay their own family members for rebellion against God. For this, the Levites were appointed as the only ones who would serve in God's Temple, rather than the firstborn from every Jewish family. With this change, out of all the tribes of Israel, only one tribe was allowed to draw near to God instead of a priest from every household. (See Exodus 32-33, Numbers 3.)

After one year in the wilderness, it was time for Israel to inherit the Promised Land. Moses sent twelve spies into the Promised Land to bring back a report. Although all twelve agreed that it was a good land, only two of the spies believed that God was able to give it to them. The people of Israel rejected the report of the two spies and agreed with the unbelief of the ten spies. As a consequence for this rebellion, God was again ready to disinherit the people of Israel and start over with only Moses by multiplying Moses' descendants into a new generation which would inherit His promises and His Kingdom. However, Moses interceded for Israel. Therefore, God decreed that Israel would have to stay in the wilderness for forty years until the entire generation from twenty years of age and older had died. None of them would be allowed to inherit the Promised Land. Their children, who had no knowledge of good and evil, would possess it. After God told them of this consequence, they rebelled again by trying to take the Promised Land for themselves. This attempt was miserably defeated and eventually, their entire generation died in the wilderness, except for the two spies who had trusted in God's faithfulness. (See Numbers 13-14, Deuteronomy 1:29.)

Towards the end of their wilderness journey, when they were about to engage in battle on their way to inheriting the Promised Land, the Israelites again rebelled against God and Moses. By this point, the former generation had almost entirely passed on, and the new generation became impatient, thinking that God had brought them this far only to let them die without fulfilling His promises. For this, God unleashed venomous serpents against them which bit them with lethal bites. However,

God instructed Moses to lift up a pole with a bronze replica of the serpent on it so that anyone who looked with faith at the bronze snake would be healed and would live. (See Numbers 21.)

After God gave Israel the Promised Land under Joshua's leadership, there were times when Israel did well in obeying the Torah and remained faithful to God. At other times however, they revealed the likeness of the adversary as in Adam and Eve's rebellion and failed miserably to adhere to God and His ways. When they failed, adversaries were allowed to rule over them for a time. When they cried out to God for mercy, God delivered them. During this time, the Jewish people's devotion to God and the Torah waned. Everyone did what was right in their own sight, according to their own knowledge of good and evil, and often according to the ways of the pagan nations. (See the Book of Judges.)

A Human King

Eventually, Israel asked God to give them a King so that they could be like all the other nations. In this, they were partially right and partially wrong. They knew they were supposed to be a Kingdom for God on the earth, but they were rejecting God as their rightful King.

Nevertheless, God granted their request and appointed a man named Saul from the tribe of Benjamin as the first King of Israel. With their first human King, would Israel fulfill their destiny as a Kingdom of God on the earth? No. Saul did well at first in remaining true to God. Soon however, he disobeyed God's instructions, and the Kingdom was taken from him and given to David, a simple shepherd boy from Bethlehem of the tribe of Judah. (See 1 Samuel 1-15.)

*1 Samuel 13:13-14 - "You have done a foolish thing," Samuel said. "**You have not kept the command the LORD your God gave you; if you had, he would have established your kingdom over Israel for all time. But now your kingdom will not endure**; the LORD has sought out a man after his own heart and appointed him ruler of his people, because you have not kept the LORD's command."*

*1 Samuel 15:28 - Samuel said to him, "**The LORD has torn the kingdom of Israel from you today and has given it to one of your neighbors**--to one better than you."*

David was a man after God's own heart. God entered into covenant with David through which He exclusively transferred the right to the keys to the Kingdom of God to one of David's sons and his direct descendants. Even though it was the tribe of Levi who was chosen to minister to God in His earthly Tabernacle and Temple, God's selection of David was consistent with the prophecy of Jacob that the Messiah of Israel would come through the tribe of Judah. Judah would hold the scepter of God's Kingdom. God would be a Father to David's descendant, the Messiah, establishing His Kingdom forever.

*2 Samuel 7:12-16 - "When your days are over and you rest with your ancestors, I will raise up your offspring to succeed you, your own flesh and blood, and **I will establish his kingdom**. He is the one who* *will build a house for my Name, and **I will establish the throne of his kingdom forever. I will be his father, and he will be my son**. When he does wrong, I will punish him with a rod wielded by men, with floggings inflicted by human hands. But my love will never be taken away from him, as I took it away from Saul, whom I removed from before you. **Your house and your kingdom will endure forever before me; your throne will be established forever**."*

*Psalm 89:3-4, 27-29, 35-37 - You [the LORD] said, "I have made a covenant with my chosen one, I have sworn to David my servant, '**I will establish your [David's] line forever and make your [David's] throne firm through all generations**.' ... And I [the LORD] will appoint him [David's descendant, the Messiah] to be my firstborn, the most exalted of the kings of the earth**. I will maintain my love to him forever, and my covenant with him will never fail. I will establish his line forever, his throne as long as the heavens endure. ... Once for all, I have sworn by my holiness--and I will not lie to David--that **his line will continue forever and his throne endure before me like the sun; it will be established forever like the moon, the faithful witness in the sky**."*

*Isaiah 22:22-23 ESV - "And **I will place on his [the Messiah's] shoulder the key of the house of David [keys to the Kingdom of God]**. He shall open, and none shall shut; and he shall shut, and none shall open. And I will fasten him like a peg in a secure place, and **he will become a throne of honor to his father's house**."*

Unfortunately, soon after this, David made some royal missteps against the Torah and God's ways. God would have been justified in putting David to death for his sins and revoking His covenant with David, but He never did. Even though there were short-term consequences within David's family and in Israel for David's errors, David was quick and sincere about admitting his faults, turning from his sins, genuinely entrusting himself to the Lord's mercy, and offering the blood sacrifices required by the Torah for the atonement of his soul. In spite of his sins, this is what made David a man after God's own heart.

Then, during the times of David's son Solomon, Israel had a taste of what it would be like to be the Kingdom designed by God to bear His image and be a blessing to the whole world. The Temple of the God of Israel was built in Jerusalem on the very same mountain where Abraham had offered Isaac and trusted in God's provision for his descendants and God's Kingdom. Because Solomon recognized the high importance that God placed on the blood of sacrifices offered on His altar and the atoning power of blood for the sins of the people, he offered 22,000 oxen and 120,000 sheep and goats, shedding massive amounts of blood to dedicate the Temple of God. (See 1 Kings 8:63.) The glory of God filled the Temple, and the people of Israel were esteemed as the only people on earth in covenant with the Most High God, Creator of the Universe. People came from far and wide to worship the God of Israel and to hear the God-given wisdom of Solomon. This was the closest Israel had come so far to having a Kingdom which bore God's image and blessed the whole world.

However, Solomon was neglectful about obedience to God's instructions and gave way to rebellion in his own life, particularly through intermarriage with Gentile women who led him astray by their worldly ways. This insubordination resulted in the Kingdom of Israel being split in two after his lifetime. Ten out of the twelve tribes of Israel abandoned David's royal line to form the northern kingdom, while two tribes carried on with David's line to form the southern kingdom.

Both the northern and the southern kingdoms began to adopt the practices of the pagans in the land. In addition to this, the kings of the northern kingdom erected their own altars, created their own festivals to God, and appointed their own priests from the common people. These activities were in direct rebellion against God's explicit instructions that Jerusalem, the place where He had chosen to put His name forever, was the only place that sacrifices could be offered to Him. These things were also against the rules of the Torah, which gives clear instructions about God's appointed feasts, priests, and Levites. The northern kingdom's rebellion against God and His ways went from bad to worse until the kingdom was scattered among the nations by the Assyrians in 722 B.C.E. in accordance with the consequences outlined in the Torah. The kings of the southern kingdom had a little more success. Some were good, some bad; some were faithful, and some wretched. But eventually their collective disobedience led to their scattering and exile to Babylon, in accordance with the consequences outlined in the Torah. Jerusalem was overthrown by Nebuchadnezzar, and the Temple of the God of Israel was destroyed on the 9th of Av, in the year 586 B.C.E.

In the centuries leading up to the destruction and exile of the northern and southern kingdoms, God faithfully sent Prophets to both kingdoms to warn God's people of what would happen to them if they did not repent, turn to Him as their one and only King, and keep His ways. This included Elijah, a powerful Prophet of God who stood up against the false practices instituted by the king of Israel to turn the hearts of the Jewish people back to God. Unfortunately, through the years, the Jewish people not only refused to heed the words and warnings of God's Prophets, but they persecuted and killed most of the Prophets for saying things that they didn't want to hear. The Jews continued living their lives as they pleased, including blending in with the pagan cultural norms of the Gentiles rather than obeying the Torah. In due time, the words of the Prophets came to pass. Just like God's banishment of Adam and Eve from Eden into exile, God ejected His people from the Promised Land and scattered them to the four corners of the earth. (See the Books of Kings and Chronicles.)

A New Covenant

In spite of their banishment from the Land, God's Prophets revealed God's plans and promises for the future of Israel. The same God who had given prophetic hope of restoration for Adam and Eve after their expulsion from Eden, now gave prophetic promises to Israel, including that God would bring the exiles back to the Promised Land. (See the previous section of the book.) More significantly, God promised to enter into a New Covenant with Israel which would prevent this cycle from recurring again.

Jeremiah 31:31-37 - "The days are coming," *declares the LORD, "when **I will make a new covenant with the people of Israel and with the people of Judah. It will not be like the covenant I made with their ancestors when I took them by the hand to lead them out of Egypt, because they broke my covenant, though I was a husband to them,"** declares the LORD. "This is the covenant I will make with the people of Israel after that time," declares the LORD. "**I will put my law in their minds and write it on their hearts. I will be their God, and they will be my people**. No longer will they teach their neighbor, or say to one another, 'Know the LORD,' because they will all know me, from the least of them to the greatest," declares the LORD. "**For I will forgive their wickedness and will remember their sins no more**." This is what the LORD says, he who appoints the sun to shine by day, who decrees the moon and stars to shine by night, who stirs up the sea so that its waves roar--the LORD Almighty is his name: "Only if these decrees vanish from my sight," declares the LORD, "will Israel ever cease being a nation before me." This is what the LORD says: "**Only if the heavens above can be measured and the foundations of the earth below be searched out will I reject all the descendants of Israel because of all they have done,"** declares the LORD.*

The New Covenant between God and Israel would not be like the covenant God had established with them at Sinai when He gave the Torah through Moses. Due to the fact that they had proved again and again to be incapable of adhering to God's ways, obeying the Torah, and heeding the warnings and directives of His Prophets, God would extend a great mercy to His chosen people through the New Covenant. The Prophets promised that through this New Covenant between God and Israel, God would write the Torah on their hearts and give them a new heart and a new spirit. God would even place His own Spirit within them so that they would no longer be inclined toward Adam-and-Eve-style rebellion. Additionally, God would forgive all of their disobedience to the Torah and no longer remember their sins against them. This would mean that there would no longer be any divinely instituted consequence for their error and rebellion, including the sins of their ancestors. This way, God's people would be able to obey Him from the heart and fulfill their God-given destiny as an image-bearing Kingdom of God and blessing to all the earth.

Ezekiel 36:26-27 - "I will give you a new heart and put a new spirit in you; I will remove from you your heart of stone and give you a heart of flesh. And I will put my Spirit in you and move you to follow my decrees and be careful to keep my laws."

Ezekiel 11:19-21 - "I will give them an undivided heart and put a new spirit in them; I will remove from them their heart of stone and give them a heart of flesh. Then they will follow my decrees and be careful to keep my laws. They will be my people, and I will be their God. But as for those whose hearts are devoted to their vile images and detestable idols, I will bring down on their own heads what they have done," declares the Sovereign LORD.

However, the Prophets also warned that anyone who does not enter into the New Covenant will continue to be judged according to the Torah, God's existing covenant with Israel through Moses. This means that their sins and the sins of their ancestors will continue to be remembered against them as Israel had already experienced.

Messiah, the Righteous King of Israel

In the same way that God's existing covenants were established through God's chosen men Noah, Abraham, Moses, and David, God promised through His Prophets that this New Covenant would be given to Israel through His Servant, the Messiah.

The Messiah is the Righteous Branch and Servant of God who becomes the New Covenant between God and the Jewish people to draw them back to obedience to God so that they can fulfill their destiny as His image-bearing Kingdom people. According to the prophecies, the Spirit of the Lord would continually guide the Messiah and He would bring with Him the power of God for healing the sick and working miracles in the earth. Since the Messiah would crush the head of the ancient serpent and possess the keys to the Kingdom of God, Israel would be able to become a blessing to the whole earth and extend the Kingdom of God even to Gentiles.

*Isaiah 11:1-2 - **A shoot will come up from the stump of Jesse; from his roots a Branch will bear fruit. The Spirit of the LORD will rest on him--the Spirit of wisdom and of understanding, the Spirit of counsel and of might, the Spirit of the knowledge and fear of the LORD.***

*Isaiah 35:3-6 - Strengthen the feeble hands, steady the knees that give way; say to those with fearful hearts, **"Be strong, do not fear; your God [the Messiah] will come**, he will come with vengeance; with divine retribution he [the Messiah] will come to save you." Then will **the eyes of the blind be opened and the ears of the deaf unstopped. Then will the lame leap like a deer, and the mute tongue shout for joy.** Water will gush forth in the wilderness and streams in the desert.*

*Isaiah 42:1-7 - **"Here is my servant [the Messiah], whom I uphold, my chosen one in whom I delight; I will put my Spirit on him, and he will bring justice to the nations**. He will not shout or cry out, or raise his voice in the streets. A bruised reed he will not break, and a smoldering wick he will not snuff out. **In faithfulness he will bring forth justice; he will not falter or be discouraged till he establishes justice on earth**. In his teaching the islands will put their hope." This is what God the LORD says--the Creator of the heavens, who stretches them out, who spreads out the earth all that springs from it, who gives breath to its people, and life to those who walk on it: **"I, the LORD, have called you in righteousness; I will*** *take hold of your hand. I will keep you and will* *make you to be a covenant for the people and a* *light for the Gentiles, to open eyes that are blind, to* *free captives from prison and to release from the* *dungeon those who sit in darkness."*

Isaiah 49:5-9 - And now the LORD says--he who *formed me [the Messiah] in the womb to be his* *servant to bring Jacob back to him and gather* *Israel to himself, for I am honored in the eyes of the* *LORD and my God has been my strength--he says:* *"It is too small a thing for you to be my servant to* *restore the tribes of Jacob and bring back those of* *Israel I have kept. I will also make you a light for* *the Gentiles, that my salvation may reach to the* *ends of the earth." This is what the LORD says--the* *Redeemer and Holy One of Israel--to him who was* *despised and abhorred by the nation, to the servant* *of rulers: "Kings will see you and stand up, princes* *will see and bow down, because of the LORD, who* *is faithful, the Holy One of Israel, who has chosen* *you." This is what the LORD says: "In the time of my* *favor I will answer you, and in the day of salvation I* *will help you; I will keep you and will make you to* *be a covenant for the people, to restore the land* *and to reassign its desolate inheritances, to say to* *the captives, 'Come out,' and to those in darkness,* *'Be free!'" They will feed beside the roads and find* *pasture on every barren hill.*

Isaiah 61:1-3 - "The Spirit of the Sovereign LORD *is on me [the Messiah], because the LORD has* *anointed me to proclaim good news to the poor. He has sent me to bind up the brokenhearted, to proclaim freedom for the captives and release from darkness for the prisoners, to proclaim the year of the LORD's favor and the day of vengeance of our God, to comfort all who mourn, and provide for those who grieve in Zion--to bestow on them a crown of beauty instead of ashes, the oil of joy instead of mourning, and a garment of praise instead of a spirit of despair. They will be called oaks of righteousness, a planting of the LORD for the display of his splendor."*

Even in the midst of their exile, God continually reassured His people that He will never reject all of the descendants of Israel because of their rebellion. Instead, He would send the Messiah to establish justice in the earth as God's anointed King whom has been promised from the beginning and who lives in perfect righteousness and obedience to God, a standard that no one else has been able to live up to. (See Isaiah, Jeremiah, Ezekiel, Daniel, and the rest of the Prophets.)

Returned Exiles Prepare for their King

At the appointed time after the Babylonian exile, God allowed many of the scattered Jews to return to the Promised Land. They were able to rebuild a Temple in Jerusalem and God allowed them to experience some level of spiritual re-awakening. However, this Temple was not as grand as Solomon's had been, and the glory of God never filled it. Plus, the Jewish people remained under the authority of a foreign King and were not re-established as an independent nation. Also, many Jews were still scattered in the nations and even the returned exiles became more focused on their own personal affairs of home and business than the things of God and obedience to the Torah. (See Ezra, Nehemiah, Haggai.)

Out of fear that the increasing lukewarm devotion of Jewish people to God and the Torah would result in a repeat of God's judgment against the Jewish people, a group of religious leaders, scribes, and scholars formed in 167 B.C.E. and called themselves Pharisees. Later, in the first century B.C.E. the Houses of Hillel and Shammai were established to train Jewish men in Jewish matters. These men instituted many rules which either added regulations for obeying the Torah or negated the need to adhere to the Torah as strictly as it was written by Moses. Plus, they did so in spite of the fact that Moses explicitly commanded that nothing be added to his words in the Torah or taken from them and the people of Israel agreed to have curses come upon them if they did not adhere to the Torah as Moses commanded. (See Deuteronomy 27:26.)

*Deuteronomy 4:2 - **Do not add to what I command you and do not subtract from it**, but keep the commands of the LORD your God that I give you.*

*Deuteronomy 12:32 - See that you do all I command you; **do not add to it or take away from it**.*

Some of the rules instituted at this time are still observed by Jews all over the world because they became the basis for Rabbinic Judaism as it exists today. However, these regulations are not the New Covenant which God promised to Israel but are the traditions of men and scholars and were put in place for Jewish people everywhere to observe as they await the Messiah—the coming King of Israel.

Eventually, when the Roman Empire took over the world, Herod was placed over the Jews as their ruler, and called himself the King of the Jews. Herod's family were Gentile converts to Judaism, but his religious commitment was a cause for speculation. Although he was most certainly not the promised King and Messiah of Israel, he did a massive re-construction of the Temple of God in Jerusalem. This Temple is said to have been even more grand and opulent than Solomon's Temple but, regardless of its fantastic outward appearance, the glory of God never filled this Temple the way it had filled Solomon's. In addition to allowing the construction of this magnificent Temple, Rome allowed the Jewish people some level of religious freedom to follow the Torah and rule themselves on religious matters. Therefore, it was in Herod's Temple that the Great Sanhedrin met every day except on festivals and Shabbat, ruling over the Jewish people to the extent that they had authority from Rome to do so.

During this time, the Jewish people did not resemble a Kingdom at all. Many of them were still scattered in the nations, and even in the Promised Land, they were subjected to Gentiles ruling over them. Plus, instead of a King of their own, they had a religious court generating more and more rulings and rules for how good Jews needed to live. The purpose of Israel to be a blessing to Gentiles had all but been forgotten as they continued to live under the suppression of Rome. However, there was eager expectation for the Messiah's arrival, partly because of the desire for liberation from foreign kings but mostly because of the words of God's Prophets.

The Timeline for the Messiah's Arrival

According to the Book of Daniel, which was written during the time of the Jewish people's exile in Babylon, God gave an exact timeline for the arrival of the Messiah. Daniel was reading the prophecies of Jeremiah and understood that God had ordained seventy years of exile in Babylon for the Jewish people. Moreover, Daniel calculated that the seventy years was almost complete. So, Daniel prayed and fasted and confessed Israel's disobedience to the Torah and asked God for mercy and restoration—a prayer we looked at in the last section. During this time of prayer and fasting, the angel Gabriel appeared to Daniel to give him insight and understanding about the things to come and the arrival of the Messiah.

*Daniel 9:24-27 - **Seventy "sevens" are decreed for your people and your holy city to finish transgression, to put an end to sin, to atone for wickedness, to bring in everlasting righteousness, to seal up vision and prophecy and to anoint the Most Holy Place.** Know and understand this: **From the time the word goes out to restore and rebuild Jerusalem until the Anointed One, the ruler, comes, there will be seven "sevens," and sixty-two "sevens."** It will be rebuilt with streets and a trench, but in times of trouble. **After the sixty-two "sevens," the Anointed One will be put to death [cut off, excommunicated/karet] and will have nothing.** The people of the ruler who will come will destroy the* *city and the sanctuary. The end will come like a flood: War will continue until the end, and desolations have been decreed.* **He will confirm a covenant with many for one "seven." In the middle of the "seven" he will put an end to sacrifice and offering.** *And at the temple he will set up an abomination that causes desolation, until the end that is decreed is poured out on him.*

In the days of Daniel's writing and the way that the Great Sanhedrin would have been calculating, a "seven" (some translations call it a "week") refers to a period of seven years. In those times, a year was 360 days based on the lunar calendar. The "time the word goes out to restore and rebuild Jerusalem" took place in 445 B.C.E. when, in the twentieth year of King Artaxerxes of Persia, a decree was issued which permitted the rebuilding of the Temple of God in Jerusalem. (See Nehemiah 2:1-5.) Gabriel revealed to Daniel that starting from the time of this decree, a timeline of seventy sevens, or 490 years, which was unequally divided into 7 sevens, 62 sevens, and one more seven which is divided into two half-sevens. The Messiah would be cut off after the 7 sevens and 62 sevens, or 483 years, equaling 173,800 days. Accordingly, in the way they would have calculated, 445 B.C.E. plus 173,800 days reveals that the Messiah would be put to death around the year 33 C.E.

The Prophet Isaiah also gave some insight into what the death or "cutting off" of the Messiah was going to entail. The Messiah, the Righteous Branch, would suffer for the sins of the unrighteous.

Isaiah 53:2-12 ESV - For he grew up before him like

a young plant, and like a root out of dry ground; he had no form or majesty that we should look at him, and no beauty that we should desire him. **He was despised and rejected by men; a man of sorrows, and acquainted with grief**; and as one from whom men hide their faces he was despised, and **we esteemed him not**. **Surely he has borne our griefs and carried our sorrows; yet we esteemed him stricken, smitten by God, and afflicted. But he was pierced for our transgressions; he was crushed for our iniquities; upon him was the chastisement that brought us peace, and with his wounds we are healed. All we like sheep have gone astray; we have turned--every one--to his own way; and the LORD has laid on him the iniquity of us all.** He was oppressed, and he was afflicted, yet he opened not his mouth; **like a lamb that is led to the slaughter, and like a sheep that before its shearers** is silent, so he opened not his mouth. By oppression and judgment he was taken away; and as for his generation, who considered that **he was cut off out of the land of the living, stricken for the transgression of my people**? And they made his grave with the wicked and with a rich man in his death, although he had done no violence, and there was no deceit in his mouth. **Yet it was the will of the LORD to crush him**; he has put him to grief; **when his soul makes an offering for guilt**, he shall see his offspring; he shall prolong his days; the will of the LORD shall prosper in his hand. **Out of the anguish of his soul he shall see and be satisfied; by his knowledge shall the righteous one, my servant,** *make many to be accounted righteous [justifying them before God], and he shall bear their iniquities. Therefore I will divide him a portion with the many, and he shall divide the spoil with the strong, because he poured out his soul to death and was numbered with the transgressors; yet he bore the sin of many, and makes intercession for the transgressors.*

According to the Prophet Isaiah, God's righteous Messiah would be rejected by the Jewish people who had each turned away from God like sheep without a shepherd, in the likeness of Adam and Eve's rebellion. Even though the Messiah would be innocent of evil, He would be inflicted with the punishment of God that the people deserved. Like a spotless sacrificial lamb, the sins of the people would be laid upon the Messiah, and His soul would become an offering of atonement for their souls.

According to the Prophet Jeremiah, the Messiah's righteous atonement would grant His followers a status of righteousness before God. This was something that the Jewish people had consistently proven was unattainable by human effort.

*Jeremiah 23:5-6 NKJV - "Behold, [the] days are coming," says the LORD, "That **I will raise to David a Branch of righteousness; A King shall reign and prosper, And execute judgment and righteousness in the earth.** In His days Judah will be saved, And Israel will dwell safely; Now this [is] His name by which **He will be called: THE LORD OUR RIGHTEOUSNESS."***

According to the Prophet Malachi, the Messiah's ministry would be preceded by a forerunner. This messenger would prepare the way for the Messiah by coming in the spirit of Elijah, the great Prophet of Israel who had turned the hearts of the Jewish people back to God in his day.

*Malachi 3:1 - "**I will send my messenger, who will prepare the way before me**. Then suddenly the Lord you are seeking will come to his temple; the messenger of the covenant, whom you desire, will come," says the LORD Almighty.*

*Malachi 4:5 - "Se**e, I will send the prophet Elijah to you before that great and dreadful day of the LORD comes**."*

Messiah's Birth

At the exact time prophesied by Daniel; Gabriel, the same angel who had visited Daniel, visited the earth again. This time Gabriel came to visit a young Jewish woman from the tribe of Judah named Miriam who was betrothed to Yosef, both of whom were direct descendants of King David. Similar to how angels had told Abraham and Sarah about their upcoming miracle birth, Gabriel told Miriam that even though she was a virgin, she would conceive a child by the power of the Spirit of the LORD, and she was to name Him Yeshua. The name Yeshua means God saves, because Miriam's son would save the people from their sins. (See Matthew 1 and Luke 1, 3:23-38.)

*Isaiah 7:14 - Therefore the Lord himself will give you a sign: **The virgin will conceive and give birth*** *to a son, and will call him Immanuel [which means God with us.]*

In accordance with the prophecies and promises of the Scriptures, God came to dwell with His people. Because Yeshua was conceived by the power of the Spirit of the LORD, the Holy Spirit, God was His Father. Yeshua was also the seed of a woman descended from Eve—the One who would crush the head of the adversary. Yeshua was formed in the womb in God's exact likeness to be God's perfect human image-bearer and King to reign on the eternal throne promised to David.

*Luke 1:32-35 – [Gabriel speaking to Miriam]: "He [Yeshua] will be great and will be called the Son of the Most High. **The Lord God will give him the throne of his father David, and he will reign over Jacob's descendants forever; his kingdom will never end.**" "How will this be," Miriam asked the angel, "since I am a virgin?" The angel answered, "The Holy Spirit will come on you, and the power of the Most High will overshadow you. **So the holy one to be born will be called the Son of God.**"*

This son of Miriam was born in Bethlehem, the prophesied birthplace of the Messiah according to the Scriptures and all of the priests and Torah scribes in that day. (See Micah 5:2 and Matthew 2:4-6) He is the One anointed by God to bring the Jewish people into the New Covenant promised to Israel and make a way for their sins to be remembered no more.

*Isaiah 9:6-7 - **For to us a child is born, to us a son is given, and the government will be on his***

89

shoulders. And he will be called Wonderful Counselor, Mighty God, Everlasting Father, Prince of Peace. Of the greatness of his government and peace there will be no end. *He will reign on David's throne and over his kingdom, establishing and upholding it with justice and righteousness from that time on and forever.* The zeal of the LORD Almighty will accomplish this.

Yeshua was circumcised on the eighth day in accordance with the Torah and grew up to manhood in submission to His Jewish parents. Because the Holy Spirit guided Him from the heart, He never rebelled against God like Adam and never disobeyed God's ways or laws as given in the Torah, intentionally or unintentionally. From the womb, Yeshua was perfectly righteous and blameless before God, and God walked with Him.

Elijah Comes

Before the start of Yeshua's ministry, a man named Yohanan went throughout the wilderness of the Jordan in the spirit of Elijah. He cried out, "Repent for the Kingdom of God is at hand!" and administered mikvehs (ritual cleansing by submersion in water) to symbolically wash people from their sins. For this, people referred to Yohanan as "the Immerser." Yohanan openly admitted that he was not the Messiah but that he was the voice in the wilderness preparing the way for the Messiah to come. (See Isaiah 40:3.) Later, when Yohanan saw Yeshua, he cried out, "Behold, the Lamb of God who takes away the sins of the world," acknowledging Yeshua as the Messiah of Israel. (See John 1.)

Messiah's Kingdom Message

Throughout His ministry, Yeshua had one simple and clear message, "Repent, for the Kingdom of God is at hand!" Yeshua reached out exclusively to Jewish people teaching in synagogues throughout Israel, in the Galilee region, and at the Temple in Jerusalem, encouraging them to turn from their sinful ways and live for God. (See Isaiah 9:1-2.) In every circumstance Yeshua faced, He said only what God was saying and did only what God was doing because He had the Spirit of God inside of Him to guide Him. Yeshua demonstrated God's likeness, holiness, righteousness, and mercy. His words, teachings, and actions demonstrated greater God-given wisdom than that of King Solomon.

Yeshua spoke almost exclusively about the Kingdom of God and He taught His followers that the Kingdom of God was the absolute top priority and the thing to be sought after above all else.

> *Matthew 6:31-33 - **So do not worry, saying, "What shall we eat?" or "What shall we drink?" or "What shall we wear?"** For the pagans run after all these things, and your heavenly Father knows that you need them. **But seek first his kingdom and his righteousness, and all these things will be given to you as well.***

Yeshua also demonstrated the power of the Kingdom of God by healing the sick, cleansing lepers, casting out demons, and raising the dead. In a similar way to how God had worked miracles for Moses so that the Jewish people would believe that he was God's appointed servant, God worked miracles through Yeshua. In accordance with the prophecies pointing to the Messiah, the sick were healed, the blind saw, the deaf heard, the lame walked, the dead were raised, and good news was proclaimed to the poor. He sent His followers out to reach the Jewish people, proclaiming the message of the Kingdom of God and doing the miraculous works that He did in order to reveal that the Kingdom of God had come near.

> *Luke 10:8-12 - "When you enter a town and are welcomed, eat what is offered to you.* ***Heal the sick who are there and tell them, 'The kingdom of God has come near to you.'*** *But when you enter a town and are not welcomed, go into its streets and say, 'Even the dust of your town we wipe from our feet as a warning to you. Yet* ***be sure of this: The kingdom of God has come near****.' I tell you, it will be more bearable on that day for Sodom than for that town."*

Yeshua was not on a self-promotional "Messiah Tour of Israel" but rather, preferred to keep His identify concealed so that only those who had a heart to perceive His message as coming from God would believe Him and follow Him. Those who recognized this discerned that Yeshua spoke the words of eternal life which were from God and not the words of the knowledge of good and evil or rules and regulations like the religious leaders.

This said, Yeshua never rebelled against the Torah nor did He encourage anyone else to do so. Yeshua even said that the Torah scribes and teachers who understand the things of the Kingdom of God have special advantages over those who do not have knowledge of the Torah.

> *Matthew 5:17-20 -* **"Do not think that I have come to abolish the Law or the Prophets; I have not come to abolish them but to fulfill them.** *For truly I tell you, until heaven and earth disappear, not the smallest letter, not the least stroke of a pen, will by any means disappear from the Law until everything is accomplished. Therefore* **anyone who sets aside one of the least of these commands and teaches others accordingly will be called least in the kingdom of heaven, but whoever practices and teaches these commands will be called great in the kingdom of heaven.** *For I tell you that* **unless your righteousness surpasses that of the Pharisees and the teachers of the law, you will certainly not enter the kingdom of heaven."**

> *Matthew 13:52 - He [Yeshua] said to them,* **"Therefore every teacher of the law who has become a disciple in the kingdom of heaven is like the owner of a house who brings out of his storeroom new treasures as well as old."**

Moreover, Yeshua raised the standard of obedience to God to be one that cut through to the motives of the heart, not just a measure of external actions. According to His teachings, looking at a woman lustfully is the same as committing the act of adultery and anger against someone is the same as committing the act of murder. The only way for His followers to be able to live up to such an impossible standard would be for them to be reborn by the Spirit of the Lord in keeping with the New

Covenant. Without an internal renovation of the human heart and spirit in order to purify character and morality at their deepest levels, no person would ever be able to attain the standard of Yeshua's teachings. For this, Yeshua promised that the Holy Spirit, the Spirit of truth, would be sent from Heaven to dwell inside His followers to enable them to live out His commands and teachings and participate in the Kingdom of God.

John 3:3-6 - Yeshua replied, "Very truly I tell you, **no one can see the kingdom of God unless they are born again."** *"How can someone be born when they are old?" Nicodemus [a Pharisee] asked. "Surely they cannot enter a second time into their mother's womb to be born!" Yeshua answered,* **"Very truly I tell you, no one can enter the kingdom of God unless they are born of water and the Spirit. Flesh gives birth to flesh, but the Spirit gives birth to spirit.***"*

John 14:15-17 - **"If you love me, keep my commands.** *And I will ask the Father [God], and he will* **give you another advocate to help you and be with you forever--the Spirit of truth.** *The world cannot accept him, because it neither sees him nor knows him. But* **you know him, for he lives with you and will be in you.***"*

All of this is to say that what God desired from the beginning of mankind for the establishment of His Kingdom on the earth is childlike trust and obedience to His commands from the depths of the heart. This kind of humble submission and faith in God is what God had found in Abraham and is exactly what Yeshua taught.

*Matthew 18:1-4 - At that time the disciples came to Yeshua and asked, **"Who, then, is the greatest in the kingdom of heaven?"** He called a little child to him, and placed the child among them. **And he said: "Truly I tell you, unless you change and become like little children, you will never enter the kingdom of heaven. Therefore, whoever takes the lowly position of this child is the greatest in the kingdom of heaven."***

Yeshua's followers would only be able to fulfill this when the Holy Spirit was sent to dwell inside of them, in accordance with the New Covenant. This would change their hearts away from Adam and Eve's likeness back to the likeness of God.

Messiah's Authority

Yeshua's followers, who were all Jewish, came from every kind of Jewish household and lifestyle. They regarded the depth of Yeshua's understanding of the Scriptures, His miracles in healing the sick, commanding the weather, multiplying food to feed hungry people, and His mercy and compassion for people as confirmation that He was the Son of God. They openly recognized and acknowledged Yeshua as the Messiah, the promised Anointed One of God, and the Prophet like Moses whom Israel must listen to. This revelation of Yeshua's identity was the foundation upon which God would be able to build His Kingdom in the earth.

*Matthew 16:16-20 – Shimon Cephas answered, **"You are the Messiah, the Son of the living God."** Yeshua replied, **"Blessed are you, Shimon Bar***

Jonah, for this was not revealed to you by flesh and blood, but by my Father in heaven. And I tell you that you are Cephas, and on this rock I will build my congregation, and the gates of Hades will not overcome it. I will give you the keys of the Kingdom of Heaven; whatever you bind on earth will be bound in heaven, and whatever you loose on earth will be loosed in heaven." Then he ordered his disciples not to tell anyone that he was the Messiah.

The religious leaders of Israel, however, did not follow Yeshua or accept Him as the Messiah. By this time, the leaders of the Sanhedrin, who were eagerly awaiting the arrival of the Messiah due to Daniel's prophecy, had also created many rules as a supplement to the Torah which they claimed were the keys to obedience. Yeshua did not submit Himself to their rules and pointedly rejected the ones which were a contradiction of the Torah and the heart of God. (See Matthew 23.) Some of the religious leaders were so consumed with maintaining the traditions of the Jewish people and observing their religious rules that they had forgotten that being an image-bearing Kingdom for God is God's main purpose for Israel.

Additionally, some of the religious leaders, even though they desired to be freed from Roman rule, loved money and had procured positions of political power and authority for themselves by working the system. Leaders like this had turned God's house into a marketplace for personal gain and desired to "keep the peace" by maintaining the status quo. (See Isaiah 56:7.) They did not like the way Yeshua drew great crowds that acknowledged Yeshua as their King rather than the Roman Emperor. Similar to how the first generation of Israelites had repeatedly questioned and rebelled against Moses' authority and sought to return to Egypt, these religious leaders rejected Yeshua as their King while submitting to Rome's authority.

Other Jewish leaders were looking for the Messiah to come and establish His Kingdom on the Day of the Lord with great terror by overthrowing their Gentile oppressors. For them, Yeshua's teachings of humility, sacrificial love, and mercy did not fit the profile of the Messiah they were looking for. Similar to how the second generation of Israelites in the wilderness rebelled against Moses due to their inability to wait for the ultimate fulfillment of God's promises, these religious leaders rejected Yeshua because they lacked faith to see how God was fulfilling His promises right before their eyes.

All of these religious leaders conspired together to stir up false accusations against Yeshua as a deliberate attempt to prevent the Jewish people from following Him. In a move to maintain their own authority, they sought to trap Yeshua in His words and find contradictions against the Torah in His life and teachings. However, they could not because He was blameless and without fault. Then, Yeshua told this parable:

Matthew 21:33-45 - "Listen to another parable: **There was a landowner who planted a vineyard. He put a wall around it, dug a winepress in it and built a watchtower. [See Isaiah 5.]** *Then he rented the* *vineyard to some farmers and moved to another place.* **When the harvest time approached, he sent his servants to the tenants to collect his fruit.** *The tenants seized his servants; they beat one, killed another, and stoned a third. Then he sent other servants to them, more than the first time, and the tenants treated them the same way.* **Last of all, he sent his son to them. 'They will respect my son,' he said. But when the tenants saw the son, they said to each other, 'This is the heir. Come, let's kill him and take his inheritance.' So they took him and threw him out of the vineyard and killed him.** *Therefore, when the owner of the vineyard comes, what will he do to those tenants?"*

"He will bring those wretches to a wretched end," they [the religious leaders] replied, "and he will rent the vineyard to other tenants, who will give him his share of the crop at harvest time."

Yeshua said to them, "Have you never read in the Scriptures: 'The stone the builders rejected has become the cornerstone; the Lord has done this, and it is marvelous in our eyes'? **Therefore I tell you that the kingdom of God will be taken away from you and given to a people who will produce its fruit.** *Anyone who falls on this stone will be broken to pieces; anyone on whom it falls will be crushed."*

When the chief priests and the Pharisees heard Yeshua's parables, they knew he was talking about them.

From this point forward, the religious leaders sought to

put Yeshua to death.

Knowing in advance that all of this must take place, Yeshua told His followers that He would be handed over to the religious leaders, and then to the Gentiles, and would be put to death. On the night before His death, Yeshua shared a meal with His disciples. He prayed the bracha (blessing) over the bread and broke it saying, "This is my body, broken for you." Then He prayed the bracha over the wine and said, "This is my blood of the New Covenant, which is poured out for the forgiveness of sins." This was hard for His followers to understand because, like Abraham being asked to sacrifice his only son Isaac, this didn't make any sense. That night, Yeshua prayed to ask God, His Father, if there was any other way to offer atonement for His people but there was not. So, He submitted Himself to the will of God as revealed in the Scriptures, knowing that it must be fulfilled that He would be *hated without cause*. (See Psalm 69:4; John 15: 25.)

In their jealous zeal against Yeshua, the religious leaders must have completely forgotten about Daniel's prophecy because the events which followed fulfilled the words of Daniel, Isaiah, Jeremiah, Ezekiel, and the other Prophets of God. These men paid off one of Yeshua's followers to betray Him. At the appointed time, because Yeshua knew the plan of God for Him to be cut off from the land of the living in fulfillment of the Scriptures, He allowed the religious leaders to arrest Him on charges of blasphemy for claiming to be God's only Son and prophesying that the Temple would be destroyed. Of course, this wasn't blasphemy because it was true, and

He wasn't a false prophet because the Temple was eventually destroyed. Yeshua could have used His own power to stop this, or He could have called out to God to put a stop to this unjust treatment, but instead, in accordance with the Scriptures, He did not open His mouth in self-defense. Like Abraham offering Isaac, Yeshua had perfect faith in God as the source of life who had power even to raise Him from the dead in order to fulfill His promises. He trusted the prophetic promises about Himself which foretold that His death would be an offering of atonement which would establish the New Covenant between God and Israel and which would be sealed with His blood.

Messiah Cut Off

As events proceeded, the religious leaders in Jerusalem and High Priests Annas and Caiaphas, representatives of Israel on behalf of the Jewish people, declared Yeshua to be guilty as a blasphemer. He was excommunicated from Israel—literally cut off/*karet*—in accordance with the punishment for blasphemy given in the Torah and in fulfillment of Daniel's prophecy that the Messiah would be cut off. The Jews were limited, however, in that they were not allowed to carry out the death penalty. They were subject to Roman rule, and only Roman authority could put someone to death. So they brought Yeshua before Pontius Pilate and Herod, the Roman rulers over Jerusalem and Judea, demanding that Yeshua be crucified. Like Joseph's brothers had rejected Joseph and thrown him in a pit, the religious leaders rejected the idea that Yeshua was destined to rule over them and instead threw Him out. Like Esau, they failed to recognize the significance of their birthright by placing higher priority on political power, money, and matters of this world than the purposes of God's Kingdom. Like Cain, they were jealous that Yeshua's righteous life was acceptable to God and backed by God's power while their self-efforts were not.

Then, on the day of Pesach/Passover, at the same time that the Passover lambs were being slaughtered in remembrance of the way that God delivered His people from Egyptian slavery, in the very year that Daniel prophesied that the Messiah would be put to death, Yeshua HaMashiach, the eternal Passover Lamb, was slaughtered and shed His blood. On the same mountain where Abraham had offered Isaac as a sacrifice and said that God would provide for all of His promises, Yeshua the Messiah offered Himself as the only Son and Lamb of God who makes provision for atonement for the sins of the world. Yeshua was beaten, whipped, and scourged until He no longer resembled a human, and then He was hung upon a tree to die a horrifying, brutal, cursed death. (See Psalm 22.) During His crucifixion, He said to God, "Forgive them, for they know not what they do," and with His dying breath, He cried out, "It is finished!" knowing that the requirement for atonement of souls had been satisfied.

It was not just Jews who killed Him, it was all of mankind—all of the descendants of Adam and Eve who, being more inclined to the ways of the adversary, didn't want God to rule over them and be their King. Even Yeshua's own disciples abandoned Him in His death because, according to their knowledge of good and evil, this just didn't make any sense.

God's plans for His Kingdom on the earth again looked hopeless.

The King with the Keys

But on the third day, in accordance with the Scriptures, before Yeshua's body had seen any decay, God raised Him from the dead. (See Psalm 16.) Because He had lived in accordance with the Torah perfectly, He merited eternal life. Yeshua served as the eternal Passover Lamb so that He *passes over* anyone who covers their soul with His blood to protect them from the Destroyer, namely death. Like the snake on the pole that Moses held up in the wilderness, Yeshua's death on a tree became salvation and healing for all who would look to Him. Anyone who now believes in Him as the Suffering Servant and Messiah of Israel is redeemed from the curse of the Torah which means that their sins and the sins of their ancestors are no longer held against them by God.

Yeshua's resurrection proved that the offering of His soul for atonement for the souls of mankind had been accepted by God. Through His resurrection, Yeshua reversed the curse of Adam, crushed the head of Satan, and was granted the keys to the Kingdom of God. In accordance with the prophecies, the scepter of God's Kingdom would remain with the line of Judah and the seed of David. The stone the builders, the Jews, rejected had become the cornerstone and the only Mediator between God and mankind. (See Psalm 118.) Although the Gentile nations raged against Him, God bestowed upon Yeshua the right to sit at His right hand with all authority in Heaven and on earth. (See Psalms 2 and 110.)

Through all of this, God was again starting with a remnant of one Man—His Son, Yeshua, the promised Messiah of Israel. Moreover, God did this while remaining totally faithful to the Torah and every promise He had made to the Patriarchs and Prophets of Israel.

Yeshua's disciples would now be called upon to fulfill God's original purpose for mankind and for Israel for all eternity and in the world to come. Accordingly, the resurrected Yeshua showed Himself alive to His followers for forty days. He gave them the keys to the Kingdom of God and commanded them to leave behind the life they had known and go, be fruitful, and multiply in the earth by making disciples of His Kingdom. After this, He ascended to Heaven from the Mount of Olives in Jerusalem and promised that He would return to the place of His departure in order to fulfill the remaining Scriptures about the Messiah. At that time, which is still yet to come, Yeshua will judge the world, avenge all wrongdoing, and usher in the world to come.

When Yeshua ascended to and arrived in Heaven, He sat down at the right hand of God. Ten days later, the Holy Spirit was poured out from Heaven to all who believed in Yeshua who were gathered together at the Southern Steps of the Temple in Jerusalem. Similar to how a consuming fire dwelt over Sinai when the Torah was written on tablets of stone and given to Israel, flames of fire hovered over the heads of Yeshua's followers as the Torah was written on the tablets of their hearts.

*Joel 2:28-29 - "And afterward, **I will pour out my Spirit on all people**. Your sons and daughters will prophesy, your old men will dream dreams, your young men will see visions. Even on my servants, both men and women, **I will pour out my Spirit in those days.**"*

Thousands of Jews from all of the nations of the earth were in Jerusalem for Shavuot (Pentecost) and witnessed the impact of the Holy Spirit outpouring on Yeshua's followers. The crowds heard about Yeshua's death and resurrection and they too believed in Him as the Messiah of Israel. Then, similar to how the Jewish people had cleansed themselves before entering into covenant with God at Sinai, these Jews were submerged in water to be cleansed in the mikvehs right there at the Temple. After their baptisms, they were also filled with the Holy Spirit. God circumcised their hearts and fulfilled the promise of His own Spirit dwelling within those who entered into the New Covenant.

*Zechariah 12:10 - "**And I will pour out on the house of David and the inhabitants of Jerusalem a spirit of grace and supplication. They will look on me, the one they have pierced, and they will mourn for him as one mourns for an only child, and grieve bitterly for him as one grieves for a firstborn son.**"*

The New Covenant between God and Israel which had been sealed with the blood of Messiah, which He shed for the forgiveness of sins, was now fully established and functional. Followers of Yeshua now hold the keys to the Kingdom of God, bearing His image from the heart through the Holy Spirit, with delegated authority and power from Heaven for the purpose of establishing God's Kingdom in the earth. Unlike the covenant God established with Israel through Moses, and more like the covenant God had with Abraham, the righteousness through God's New Covenant with Israel would now be attained through faith. For those who believe Yeshua the Messiah, their faith is credited as righteousness. (See Habakkuk 2:4.)

In the days and years that followed, the good news of Yeshua the Messiah was initially spread only to Jews. After about ten to fifteen years, Yeshua's Jewish followers came to understand that the New Covenant was also intended to be extended to Gentiles as long as they believed in Yeshua, the Messiah of Israel. From then on and including now, anyone in any nation, Jew or Gentile alike, who confesses the name of Yeshua and believes in their heart that God raised Him from the dead will have their sins blotted out, their name written in the Book of Life, and be included in the resurrection of the righteous on the Day of Judgment. Similar to the Ark of Noah, the New Covenant offers deliverance from judgment in addition to eternal life for all who walk with God and obey Him by the power of the Holy Spirit dwelling in them.

Daniel 12:1-2 ESV - At that time shall arise Michael, the great prince who has charge of your people. ***And there shall be a time of trouble, such as never has been since there was a nation till that time. But at that time your people shall be delivered, everyone whose name shall be found*** *written in the book [Book of Life]. And many of those who sleep in the dust of the earth shall awake, some to everlasting life, and some to shame and everlasting contempt.*

At the time of Yeshua's death around 33 C.E., there was a great earthquake, and the veil in the Temple of God was torn from top to bottom. From that day forward, the Sanhedrin never met in the Temple again because the Chamber of Hewn stones where they met had been cracked beyond repair by the earthquake. (See Shabbat 15a.) Following Yeshua's death and resurrection, the religious leaders paid off Romans and Jews to spread lies that Yeshua had not actually been raised from the dead and that His body had been stolen by bandits. (See Matthew 28:11-15.) However, for the next forty years, the scarlet thread which was placed on the door of the Temple sanctuary on the Day of Atonement and which turned white when the scapegoat carrying the sins of Israel was released, never turned white again, and the miracles which the Jewish people had experienced at the Temple became inconsistent until they also stopped entirely. (See Yoma 39b.) Then, in 70 C.E., on the 9th of Av, the same day that the first Temple had been destroyed in 586 B.C.E, the Temple of God in Jerusalem was completely demolished. Not one stone remained in place. It was in this same year that the Oral Torah was assembled by the Pharisees who then disbanded in 73 C.E.

In further fulfillment of Daniel's prophecy, the Temple sacrifices and offerings were put to an end. Since the Torah does not change and is still in effect for the Jewish people, this means that according to the Torah, without a Temple on Mount Moriah in Jerusalem, there is no longer any chance of blood atonement for the souls of Jewish people which adheres to God's requirements. According to the Torah and in contrast to the common orthodox Jewish practice today, a chicken sacrificed on Yom Kippur is not an adequate atoning sacrifice and no sacrifice is acceptable anywhere other than on the Temple Mount.

The Story Continued – Side One

If you haven't figured it out by now, the person I am referring to as Yeshua the Messiah of Israel, is the person you have probably heard of as Jesus Christ. The word "Christ" is the Greek word for Messiah. In the times of Yeshua, Greek was the predominant language in the world. It was so widespread in these centuries that even the Hebrew Scriptures were translated into Greek and became known as the Septuagint.

After about ten years of the good news of Yeshua the Christ spreading to the Jews in the earth at that time, people started calling followers of Yeshua "Christians." For the next 300 years, followers of Yeshua placed their faith in Yeshua as the Messiah of Israel and were filled with the Holy Spirit, empowered to keep Yeshua's ways and live out His teachings as the Holy Spirit guided them day-by-day. Since a large portion of them were Jews who believed Yeshua to be the fulfillment of God's plan for Israel, many of Yeshua's followers continued to observe Shabbat, Rosh Chodesh (new moon/month), and the Feasts of the Lord as outlined in the Torah. In some citics, Jewish and Gentile followers of Yeshua frequently attended synagogue to hear and learn the Scriptures. Followers of Yeshua held their meetings in homes and private places because there were no churches or church buildings and because they were heavily persecuted for their faith. Christianity was outlawed, and many Christians were martyred by the Romans for claiming to follow a King other than Caesar. Some Jewish followers of Yeshua were persecuted or martyred by zealously religious Jews accusing them of blasphemy for calling Yeshua the Son of God.

The only reason that people call Yeshua "Jesus" instead of the Hebrew name given to Him at birth by His Jewish mother Miriam, is because in 313 C.E. when Constantine became the Emperor of Rome, he also appointed himself as the head of the Christian faith. While Constantine's own profession of Christian faith was often a source for speculation, he also appointed the Nicene Council over the religious matters of his Empire. The members of this council turned out to be anti-Semitic and swiftly determined that all Jewishness should be removed from Christianity, degrading the Jews as "odious" and "Christ-killers." They simply made up the name "Jesus" in place of Yeshua because Yeshua sounded too Jewish. They also changed Miriam's name to Mary and revered her as a totally chaste woman even though the Scriptures reveal that she had naturally born sons and daughters after Yeshua's miraculous birth. They tried to remove Israel from the Messiah of Israel. But in God's sight, this is not possible.

Other beliefs and practices were instituted during the time of Constantine which Yeshua and His earliest followers would not have regarded as kosher—pun intended. For example, they abandoned the Hebrew calendar and Feasts of the Lord and instead created Christmas and Easter which were and are observed on the days on which Constantine had previously celebrated festivals for worshiping Sol Invictus, the Roman god of the sun, and Ishtar, the Roman goddess of fertility. They forbid house churches and converted pagan temples into churches for Christian meetings. In keeping with the pagan temple customs, priests and leaders were appointed often through bribery or cronyism and were given titles like Father, Master, and Pope even though Yeshua had specifically instructed His followers not to call anyone father or master except God alone, and not to let anyone call them father or master. The priests became the only ones with access to the holy books while the people had no Bibles of their own to read. The priests told people what to do rather than empowering them and encouraging them to listen to the Holy Spirit for themselves the way Yeshua had. Since the leaders were pagans and were accustomed to worshiping multiple gods for sun, rain, fertility, etc., they nominated people from Christian history whom they considered to be great workers for God and revered them as saints that people could pray to when they needed something, even though Yeshua is the only God-appointed Mediator between God and man. The city of Rome was appointed as the head of the global Christian Church rather than recognizing Jerusalem as God's chosen place for His name. At the same time, Constantine's mother toured the Holy Land and built churches on every spot she deemed historically significant to Christianity. Constantine's zeal for political power mixed with his questionable profession of Christian faith diverted the focus of Christianity toward establishing a world empire rather than the Kingdom of God. Christianity became paganized, a far cry from Yeshua's life and teachings, and Yeshua's followers lost the miracle power from Heaven which put the Kingdom of God on display.

Like Joseph becoming unrecognizable to his brothers over the passage of time and seeming to be a leader for the Gentiles, it is understandable why Jews have not been able to recognize Yeshua for who He truly is—their Jewish brother. Moreover, as years of Church history progressed, the Protestant Reformation took place through which many people rebelled against some of the more egregiously wrong practices in the Church. A man named Martin Luther was the most notable reformer during this time, and he wrote many books and papers which Biblically proved the error of the ways the Christian Church had adopted. Unfortunately, Martin Luther was anti-Semitic so some of his later writings encourage people to eliminate Jews from the face of the planet even though the Holy Spirit most definitely did not reveal this to him. It was Martin Luther's writings which Hitler used to justify his actions against the Jews during World War II. The Reformation has also resulted in the establishment of various denominations or divisions within the global Christian community which are separated because of disagreements about theological matters.

The Story Continued – Side Two

On the other hand, after the destruction of Jerusalem and

the Temple in 70 C.E., the Jews who survived the Roman attack were scattered out of the Promised Land. Jerusalem's name was changed to Aelia Capitolina and the Province of Judah was renamed Syria Palaestina by the Roman Emperor in order to remove all trace of Jewishness from the land. Even more so, after the Bar Kokhba Revolt in 132-135 C.E., led by a man whom many Jews believed might be the Messiah, the Jewish people were scattered to the four corners of the earth. At that time, a temple to the Roman god Jupiter was erected on the Temple Mount in Jerusalem. The Jewish religion was outlawed, and the Romans acted without mercy toward the Jews.

Around 200 C.E., during a short window of religious reprieve under Emperor Marcus Aurelius, the Oral Torah/Law, also called the Mishnah or Jerusalem Talmud, was written down by Judah HaNasi. Although it had previously been forbidden to write down this Oral Law, HaNasi disobeyed this custom for the sake of preserving the small remnant of Jewish people that remained in the earth. He had both a fear that Jewishness would become extinct and wise perception that the window of opportunity to spread Jewish teachings under Roman rule would be short-lived.

Soon after this, Judaism and Christianity were both illegal and heavily persecuted with many devout people dying as martyrs. Then suddenly, Constantine became the Roman Emperor and declared himself to be a Christian. With this, Christianity was transformed overnight from being outlawed to being socially advantageous. By the end of Constantine's rule, it was practically against the law to not profess to be a Christian, and those who refused to convert to Christianity were forced to pay a fine. This resulted in most of the people within the borders of the Roman Empire claiming to be Christians even though they weren't. People professing to be Christians had never truly believed in their hearts that Yeshua is the Messiah of Israel and most likely, had never repented of their sins or been filled with the Holy Spirit by entering into the New Covenant. Even though they had no concept of the story of Israel or the Kingdom of God, they started claiming to do things in the name of Jesus or in the interest of the Church or for the Christian faith.

Combine the ignorance of the people with Constantine's anti-Semitic council and trouble was brewing for the Jews. This did indeed begin what became a horrific and long-lasting line of treacherous history between the Jewish people and people claiming to be working on behalf of God in the name of Christianity while persecuting God's chosen people—something Yeshua never did and would never authorize His followers to do. This said, it is easy to see how a Jewish person could believe that Christians are against them because history proves that the lines became blurred between religion, politics, government, and conquest.

Accordingly, Jewish life became more focused on survival of community either by deliberately standing out against the culture and times or by adapting Jewish beliefs to blend in with culture and times. The focus of Judaism became the preservation of traditions and teachings of the rabbis rather than actual faithfulness to

God and adhering to the Torah. The Babylonian Talmud was assembled in around 500 C.E., and the rabbinic system was firmly established following the Oral Torah and teachings of the rabbis. All of this is to say that the Jewish people were again led by their leaders into empty worship as they had been in the past.

*Isaiah 29:13 - The Lord says: **"These people come near to me with their mouth and honor me with their lips, but their hearts are far from me. Their worship of me is based on merely human rules they have been taught."***

*Isaiah 6:9 - He [the LORD] said [to Isaiah], "Go and tell this people: **'Be ever hearing, but never understanding; be ever seeing, but never perceiving.'"***

Although it is claimed that this Oral Torah goes back all the way to Moses, there is no mention of it in all of Scripture, and as I mentioned earlier, Moses explicitly commanded **not** to add to or take from his words. Moreover, because this Oral Torah was assembled after the death and resurrection of Yeshua, parts of it are written for the specific purpose of denying Yeshua as the Messiah of Israel. Stories about Yeshua are presented or framed in a way which disqualifies Him from His rightful throne. This includes referring to Him as Yeshu, which means "may his name be blotted out" as an aggressive slander against Him. Jewish leaders continued to prohibit Jews from believing Yeshua, particularly by saying that to believe Yeshua is to renounce their Jewishness, which is a lie. Nonetheless, they became violent in their rejection of their fellow

Jews who believed Yeshua and encouraged the entire Jewish community to treat Jewish followers of Yeshua as if they were dead.

Additionally, it became widely accepted that the Scriptures and the Oral Torah cannot be understood without a rabbi present to interpret it. While this creates job security for rabbis and has led to the excessive veneration of rabbis of past generations, it devalues the intelligence of the common Jew. Even though some of the rabbis were indeed brilliant men of wisdom and honor, without the Holy Spirit dwelling in them through participation in the New Covenant, their understanding and interpretation of the Scriptures is veiled and slanted. However, the asserted need for a rabbi for interpretation also gives the rabbis an easy way of rejecting any ideas which contradict their teachings even if the ideas are correct! Moreover, Synagogue services departed from the midrash/debate-style format which encouraged participation from Bar Mitzvahed men of every household and instead became more focused on painstaking adherence to the traditions of Judaism mixed with rabbinic speeches and pontifications about Jewish matters. This has resulted in several divisions within Judaism that run the gamut from the intensely strict in observance of traditions to the incredibly lax in permissiveness to a degree that unquestionably violates the Torah.

Understandably, the battle of the Jewish people to survive in the midst of hostile Gentile nations has resulted in the Jewish adoption of an "us against the Gentiles" mentality and sometimes even more specifically, an "us against the Christians" mindset. God's purpose for Israel of being His image-bearing Kingdom and a source of blessing to the Gentiles has been nearly eliminated from Jewish life. The only things that remain as a whiff of God's Kingdom God within Judaism are the supposed acceptance of the yoke of God's Kingdom through the recitation of the Shema even though nothing else about Judaism resembles a Kingdom, and the continued Jewish hope of the Messiah coming to make all things right even though this includes the expectation of His judgment against most of the rest of the world on the Jewish people's behalf.

The Faithful Remnant

I'll stop there. This brief synopsis gives you enough of an indication of the world-changing shift of events which took place after Yeshua's death and resurrection. History reveals that both Christianity and Judaism have been vulnerable to trying to become something that God never intended for mankind. God does not want people full of religion, traditions, or the knowledge of good and evil trying to make a name for themselves in the earth through their own means of attaining influence. God's purpose for mankind has always been for us to live by the power of His Spirit so that we may establish His eternal Kingdom, display His likeness through simple obedience and faithfulness, and rule over His adversary.

Religious leaders of both Judaism and Christianity have, for the most part, missed the point and purpose of God and have been poor representatives of His message, and His righteousness, holiness, and purity. The Jewish leaders have, for the most part, become consumed with seeking knowledge, observing tradition, and towing the line in their adamant refusal to consider Yeshua as the Messiah of Israel. The Christian leaders have, for the most part, been unaware of God's true purpose for Israel and the significance of the Jewishness of Yeshua and His Kingdom. Therefore, the Christian message has been altered to be one of "get saved or you're going to hell" while professing Christians live lives which bear no semblance to the God of Israel or the Torah and lack miracle power to demonstrate God's Kingdom.

But in spite of all of this, God has always maintained His faithful ones in the earth who believe that Yeshua is the Messiah of Israel, understand His teachings, live for the Kingdom of God, and experience His miracles regularly. There have been Jews who have turned from the traditions of their fathers to place their faith in Yeshua as their Messiah and enter into the New Covenant. There have been Gentile followers of Yeshua who have been courageous enough to stand up to the religious authorities and against the wrong practices in the Church. These were the ones who trust God like Abraham, often risking and sacrificing their lives to do so. These are the ones who, like the Prophets of God in the Scriptures are with Yeshua in His eternal Kingdom worshiping the Lamb of God who sits on the throne and who will judge the whole earth.

To be clear, the solution is not the eradication of religion or politics, nor is it increased "tolerance" for ways which violate God's ways and the Torah. In fact, in the times to come, there will be increasing pressure to submit to a worldwide, government-enforced religion which will violate many aspects of God's commands. However, when Yeshua returns to the earth on the Mount of Olives in Jerusalem for the Day of the LORD, He will execute judgment on the living and the dead and put an end to all of these things.

In the meantime, the only way to serve God which adheres to God's original plan for mankind and His purpose for Israel is to enter into the New Covenant through faith in Yeshua the Messiah. He is the only Mediator between God and man and the only One who can grant His followers the indwelling Holy Spirit. This is the only way that we will be able to live according to God's guidance, purity, and holiness, and devote our lives His Kingdom.

The War Today

Perhaps you have never heard the story of the Scriptures or the Kingdom of God or Yeshua the Messiah told in this manner before. Perhaps you have referred to Him with contempt as Yeshu for the blotting out of His name when the truth is that if you reject Yeshua as the Messiah, then it is your name which will be blotted out of the Book of Life. So, it is time to ask yourself: If Yeshua truly is the Messiah, the One who will return to fulfill the remaining prophecies of the Day of the LORD and judge the whole world, what will you tell Him?

Hence, we have the war for your soul. What you believe about Yeshua is a matter of eternal importance. The adversary has deliberately attempted to skew the way that Jewish people perceive Yeshua so that you will go the way of Adam and Eve and be banished from the inheritance that is rightfully yours. The ancient serpent continues to work through the knowledge of good and evil just as he has from the beginning. With his millennia of experience in tactics of war and deception, he has made the source of life appear to be the way to death and the way to death appear to be the source of life. For example, instead of a forbidden tree, the knowledge of good and evil has taken the form of erroneous religion with its rules, regulations, and empty promises. Plus, anyone's reasonable assessment of good and evil would be seriously challenged by the fact that Yeshua has been presented as the evil leader of the Gentiles who have so mercilessly persecuted the Jews throughout the centuries rather than the One sent by God to the Jewish people to extend His good-will, mercy, and eternal life through the New Covenant.

But now that you have heard the good news for yourself, what will you do about it? What are you going to believe? Who are you going to follow?

When the Jews in Yeshua's day claimed that they had access to the Kingdom of God and eternal life because they were descendants of Abraham, Yeshua informed them that biological relation to Abraham is not enough to qualify anyone for eternal life and the world to come. First of all, as Jews in Moses' covenant, righteousness is required. This is something that no one has been able to attain through their own attempts to obey the Torah. Plus, the Torah requires atoning blood sacrifices and there is presently no Temple in Jerusalem. God Himself provided the atoning sacrifice for the forgiveness of sins by sending Yeshua and so, what is required now is to *be like* Abraham—be one doing the things that Abraham did by trusting God wholeheartedly with your whole life. Just like Abraham left his father's land, household, and religious superstitions, Yeshua requires that we be willing to leave everything behind to be His disciples, seeking only after the Kingdom of God and not our own plans and purposes for our lives. This said, it is worth noting that when you place your faith in Yeshua as your Messiah, you do not lose or disown your Jewishness in any way. In fact, most Jewish followers of Yeshua discover that being Jewish finally makes sense and experience a revival of their Jewishness.

Many Jews often ask—if Messiah has come then why is there no peace on earth? It is a reasonable question, particularly given the remaining prophecies pertaining to Yeshua the Messiahs' return when He will demolish all adversaries and usher in total shalom in the world to come. However, the answer is simple: It's for your sake. Yes. There's not peace on earth yet because Messiah Yeshua is waiting for YOU to believe that He is the Messiah of Israel. In fact, He will not return until all of the true Israel is saved and Jerusalem cries out to Him, "Baruch haba b'Shem Adonai!" meaning, "Blessed is the One who comes in the name of the Lord!" (See Psalm 118:26; Matthew 23:39.) Until then, the peace Yeshua gives is in the heart and for your eternal soul. He came the first time to give His followers peace with God through His atoning blood. We benefit from peace in our hearts because we know that God is with us in this life, and we are assured of our eternal destination. God tarries in bringing forth the Day of the LORD as a great mercy to all of mankind and particularly the Jewish people in order to give more people time to repent and turn to Yeshua. This is because He knows that not even the judgment of Sodom and Gomorrah can compare to the horrendous eternal consequence of rejecting Yeshua as the Son of God and Messiah of Israel. (See Matthew 10:15.)

Consider this statement of one of the most well respected rabbis in Jewish history before his passing: *When Rabban Yochanan ben Zakkai fell ill, his disciples came to visit him. When he saw them, he began to weep. His disciples said to him, "...why do you weep?" He said to them: "...two paths are before me, one to Gan Eden (Garden of Eden) and the other to Gehinnom (hell) and I do not know upon which I am to be led—shall I not weep?"* (See the Gemara in Berakhot 28b.) If this leader of Rabbinic Judaism had no idea whether he would inherit the world to come or not, how can you place your trust his teachings? As beloved as your rabbis may be to you, they do not have the keys to the Kingdom of God or eternal life.

Please don't leave your eternal inheritance to chance because you are towing the line of the community and following "the majority rules" approach to reason. Think for yourself. Pray for yourself. Know for yourself that you have been chosen by God to inherit all that He has for you in His Kingdom.

Your Next Steps

If you believe that Yeshua is the Messiah of Israel, then your next step is to repent of rejecting Him, and ask Him to forgive you. Like Joseph extended forgiveness to his brothers when they finally recognized him even though they had rejected him and left him in a pit for dead, Yeshua is full of mercy for anyone who finally comes to see Him for who He really is. Then, repent of living your life in your own way and for your own gain. Be baptized in water like being submerged in a mikveh to wash away your sins forever, and ask Yeshua to bring you into the New Covenant, fill you with His Spirit and be your Messiah and King. Start talking to Yeshua about everything, and listen for the gentle whisper of the Holy Spirit guiding you into all truth. Acquire a Bible with a B'rit Hadasha (New Covenant/Testament), and read the words and teachings of Yeshua for yourself. Be prepared for the possibility of rejection or persecution from friends and family and from the powers that be in this world. Walk with Yeshua on a daily basis, one day at a time, standing firm until the end, and you will learn His ways, His faithfulness, and His mercy.

If you are not quite sure how to process all of this, then I challenge you to earnestly seek God and ask Him to show you without a doubt whether or not Yeshua is the Messiah of Israel. Be willing to accept whatever answer God gives you and be willing to follow through in your life and actions with whatever is revealed to you. I challenge you to do your homework, read the B'rit Hadasha for yourself, seek the truth and be willing to follow the truth wherever it leads you.

APPENDIX
Scriptures & Resources

This is merely a sample of Scriptures pertaining to the return of the Jewish people to the Land of Israel. Study them and meditate on them. Ask God to give you wisdom regarding His will for you and your family to dwell in the Land that He promised to your ancestors.

Psalm 107:2-3 - Let the redeemed of the LORD tell their story-- those he redeemed from the hand of the foe, those he gathered from the lands, from east and west, from north and south.

Psalm 147:2 - The LORD builds up Jerusalem; he gathers the exiles of Israel.

Isaiah 27:12-13 - In that day the LORD will thresh from the flowing Euphrates to the Wadi of Egypt, and you, Israel, will be gathered up one by one. And in that day a great trumpet will sound. Those who were perishing in Assyria and those who were exiled in Egypt will come and worship the LORD on the holy mountain in Jerusalem.

Isaiah 35:10 - And those the LORD has rescued will return. They will enter Zion with singing; everlasting joy will crown their heads. Gladness and joy will overtake them, and sorrow and sighing will flee away.

Isaiah 49:8-13, 22-23 - This is what the LORD says: "In the time of my favor I will answer you, and in the day of salvation I will help you; I will keep you and will make you to be a covenant for the people, to restore the land and to reassign its desolate inheritances, to say to the captives, 'Come out,' and to those in darkness, 'Be free!' They will feed beside the roads and find pasture on every barren hill. They will neither hunger nor thirst, nor will the desert heat or the sun beat down on them. He who has compassion on them will guide them and lead them beside springs of water. I will turn all my mountains into roads, and my highways will be raised up. See, they will come from afar-- some from the north, some from the west, some from the region of Aswan. Shout for joy, you heavens; rejoice, you earth; burst into song, you mountains! For the LORD comforts his people and will have compassion on his afflicted ones." ... This is what the Sovereign LORD says: "See, I will beckon to the nations, I will lift up my banner to the peoples; they will bring your sons in their arms and carry your daughters on their hips. Kings will be your foster fathers, and their queens your nursing mothers. They will bow down before you with their faces to the ground; they will lick the dust at your feet. Then you will know that I am the LORD; those who hope in me will not be disappointed."

Isaiah 51:11 - Those the LORD has rescued will return. They will enter Zion with singing; everlasting joy will crown their heads. Gladness and joy will overtake them, and sorrow and sighing will flee away.

Jeremiah 3:18 - In those days the people of Judah will join the people of Israel, and together they will come from a northern land to the land I gave your ancestors as an inheritance.

Jeremiah 23:3 - "I myself will gather the remnant of my flock out of all the countries where I have driven them and will bring them back to their pasture, where they will be fruitful and increase in number."

Jeremiah 24:6 - "My eyes will watch over them for their good, and I will bring them back to this land. I will build them up and not tear them down; I will plant them and not uproot them."

Jeremiah 30:3 - "The days are coming," declares the LORD, "when I will bring my people Israel and Judah back from captivity and restore them to the land I gave their ancestors to possess," says the LORD.

Jeremiah 31:8-14 - "See, I will bring them from the land of the north and gather them from the ends of the earth. Among them will be the blind and the lame, expectant mothers and women in labor; a great throng will return. They will come with weeping; they will pray as I bring them back. I will lead them beside streams of water on a level path where they will not stumble, because I am Israel's father, and Ephraim is my firstborn son." Hear the word of the LORD, you nations; proclaim it in distant coastlands: "He who scattered Israel will gather them and will watch over his flock like a shepherd. For the LORD will deliver Jacob and redeem them from the hand of those stronger than they. They will come and shout for joy on the heights of Zion; they will rejoice in the bounty of the LORD-- the grain, the new wine and the olive oil, the young of the flocks and herds. They will be like a well-watered garden, and they will sorrow no more. Then young women will dance and be glad, young men and old as well. I will turn their mourning into gladness; I will give them comfort and joy instead of sorrow. I will satisfy the priests with abundance, and my people will be filled with my bounty," declares the LORD.

Jeremiah 32:37-42 - "I will surely gather them from all the lands where I banish them in my furious anger and great wrath; I will bring them back to this place and let them live in safety. They will be my people, and I will be their God. I will give them singleness of heart and action, so that they will always fear me and that all will then go well for them and for their children after them. I will make an everlasting covenant with them: I will never stop doing good to them, and I will inspire them to fear me, so that they will never turn away from me. I will rejoice in doing them good and will assuredly plant them in this land with all my heart and soul." This is what the LORD says: "As I have brought all this great calamity on this people, so I will give them all the prosperity I have promised them."

Jeremiah 33:7-9 - "I will bring Judah and Israel back from captivity and will rebuild them as they were before. I will cleanse them from all the sin they have committed against me and will forgive all their sins of rebellion against me. Then this city will bring me renown, joy, praise and honor before all nations on earth that hear of all the good things I do for it; and they will be in awe and will tremble at the abundant prosperity and peace I provide for it."

Ezekiel 11:17 - Therefore say: This is what the Sovereign LORD says: "I will gather you from the nations and bring you back from the countries where you have been scattered, and I will give you back the land of Israel again."

Ezekiel 28:25-26 - This is what the Sovereign LORD says: "When I gather the people of Israel from the nations where they have been scattered, I will be proved holy through them in the sight of the nations. Then they will live in their own land, which I gave to my servant Jacob. They will live there in safety and will build houses and plant vineyards; they will live in safety when I inflict punishment on all their neighbors who maligned them. Then they will know that I am the LORD their God."

Hosea 11:10-11 - They will follow the LORD; he will roar like a lion. When he roars, his children will come trembling from the west. They will come from Egypt, trembling like sparrows, from Assyria, fluttering like doves. "I will settle them in their homes," declares the LORD.

Micah 2:12-13 - "I will surely gather all of you, Jacob; I will surely bring together the remnant of Israel. I will bring them together like sheep in a pen, like a flock in its pasture; the place will throng with people. The One who breaks open the way will go up before them; they will break through the gate and go out. Their King will pass through before them, the LORD at their head."

Micah 4:6-7 - "In that day," declares the LORD, "I will gather the lame; I will assemble the exiles and those I have brought to grief. I will make the lame my remnant, those driven away a strong nation. The LORD will rule over them in Mount Zion from that day and forever."

Zephaniah 3:20 - "At that time I will gather you; at that time I will bring you home. I will give you honor and praise among all the peoples of the earth when I restore your fortunes before your very eyes," says the LORD.

Zechariah 8:7-8 - This is what the LORD Almighty says: "I will save my people from the countries of the east and the west. I will bring them back to live in Jerusalem; they will be my people, and I will be faithful and righteous to them as their God."

Selection of Aliyah Resources

The Jewish Agency: Providing help for Jews returning to Israel and services for new Jewish immigrants to Israel. www.jewishagency.org

Aliyah Return Center: Assisting the Jewish people from the nations to return and be restored to their God-given inheritance in Israel. www.aliyahreturncenter.com

Operation Exodus: Assisting the Jewish people with mass Aliyah to Israel. International: www.operation-exodus.org USA: www.operationexodususa.org

Nefesh B'Nefesh: Aliyah resources, grants, and loans for Jews returning to Israel. www.nbn.org.il

Telfed: Assisting Jews from South Africa, Australia, and New Zealand in making Aliyah. www.telfed.org.il

Ministry of Aliyah and Integration: Responsible for the assistance that the State of Israel provides to new Aliyah immigrants. www.moia.gov.il

United Jewish Israel Appeal: Assisting Jews from United Kingdom, Ireland, and Scandinavia in making Aliyah. www.ujia.org

Association of Americans and Canadians in Israel: Providing information and guidance for new Jewish immigrants to Israel. www.aaci.org.il

Ezra International: Helping Jews from Russia, Eastern Europe, and other nations make Aliyah to Israel. www.ezrainternational.org

The Author

The author is not available for press conferences or interviews about this book. She remains in loving, hopeful prayer for the Jewish people's return and redemption. She stays focused on her work of establishing the Kingdom of God in the earth, reaching the scattered Jews in the nations, and increasing the awareness in the global Christian community of God's enduring love for the Jewish people.